SILICON CITY

SILICON CITY

SAN FRANCISCO
IN THE
LONG SHADOW
OF THE
VALLEY

CARY McCLELLAND

W. W. NORTON & COMPANY
Independent Publishers Since 1923
New York | London

Silicon City is a work of nonfiction. Some names and potentially identifying characteristics have been changed.

Copyright © 2018 by Cary McClelland

For information about permission to reproduce selections from this book, write to Permissions, W. W. Norton & Company, Inc., 500 Fifth Avenue, New York, NY 10110

For information about special discounts for bulk purchases, please contact W. W. Norton Special Sales at specialsales@wwnorton.com or 800-233-4830

Manufacturing by LSC Communications, Harrisonburg
Book design by Chris Welch
Production manager: Anna Oler

ISBN: 978-0-393-60879-3

W. W. Norton & Company, Inc., 500 Fifth Avenue, New York, N.Y. 10110
www.wwnorton.com

W. W. Norton & Company Ltd., 15 Carlisle Street, London W1D 3BS

1 2 3 4 5 6 7 8 9 0

For Lisa

See, projected through time,
For me an audience interminable.
With firm and regular step they wend, they never stop,
Successions of men, Americanos, a hundred millions,
One generation playing its part and passing on,
Another generation playing its part and passing on in its turn,
With faces turn'd sideways or backward towards me to listen,
With eyes retrospective towards me.

 —Walt Whitman, *Leaves of Grass*

This is my fair warning to the hipsters + the yuppies!!
Get the Fuck Up Out the MISSION!!
Before this Shit starts getting UGLY!!
You got 6 Months, Keep it Kickin!!
If you don't, It won't be Funny!
I Guarantee My Soldiers will GLADLY come out GUNNIN!!
Kill Hipsters + Yuppies.

 —Graffiti in San Francisco

CONTENTS

| PART II. THE SOUL OF THE CITY |

| PART III. THE BALKANIZATION OF THE BAY |

| PART IV. THE BREAKDOWN |

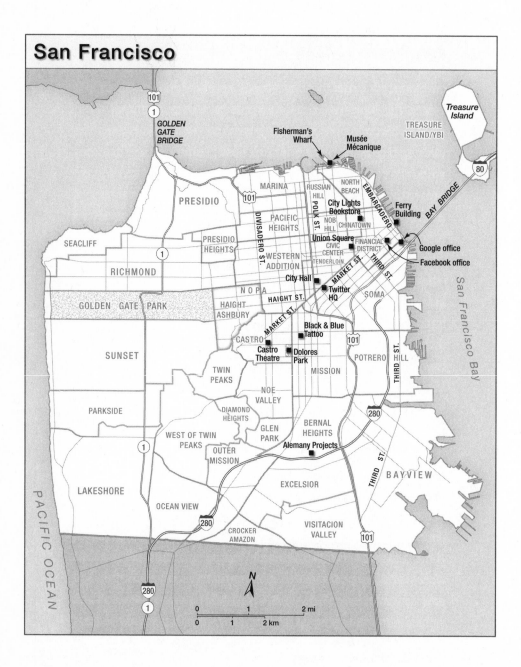

San Francisco

GOLDEN
GATE
BRIDGE

TREASURE
ISLAND/YBI

*Treasure
Island*

Fisherman's
Wharf

Musée
Mécanique

MARINA

RUSSIAN
HILL

NORTH
BEACH

PRESIDIO

PACIFIC
HEIGHTS

POLK ST.

NOB
HILL

City Lights
Bookstore

CHINATOWN

EMBARCADERO

Ferry
Building

SEACLIFF

PRESIDIO
HEIGHTS

DIVISADERO ST.

WESTERN
ADDITION

Union Square

CIVIC
CENTER

FINANCIAL
DISTRICT

Google office

RICHMOND

TENDERLOIN

MARKET ST.

THIRD ST.

Facebook office

NOPA

City Hall

HAIGHT ST.

HAIGHT ST.

Twitter
HQ

SOMA

San Francisco Bay

GOLDEN GATE PARK

HAIGHT
ASHBURY

MARKET ST.

SUNSET

CASTRO

Black & Blue
Tattoo

Castro
Theatre

Dolores
Park

POTRERO

THIRD HILL ST.

TWIN
PEAKS

MISSION

NOE
VALLEY

DIAMOND
HEIGHTS

PARKSIDE

WEST OF TWIN
PEAKS

GLEN
PARK

BERNAL
HEIGHTS

OUTER
MISSION

Alemany Projects

LAKESHORE

EXCELSIOR

THIRD ST.

BAYVIEW

OCEAN VIEW

CROCKER
AMAZON

VISITACION
VALLEY

PACIFIC OCEAN

N

0   1   2 mi

0   1   2 km

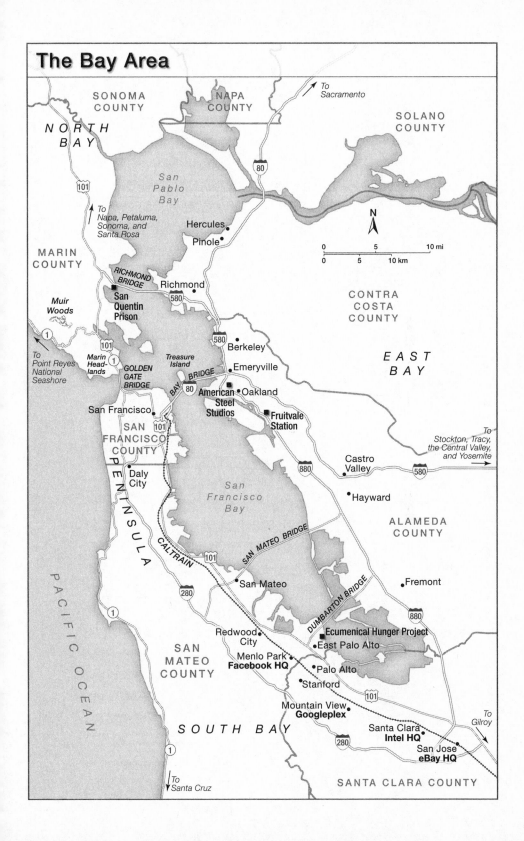

The Bay Area

Introduction

I bet you can't hit me with a quarter.

—Sign of a homeless person, standing beside the
King Street I-280 off-ramp

saw this sign as I was driving back into San Francisco one evening. Rush-hour traffic had gotten so bad it now took a half hour to clear the off-ramp. Rows of commuters all stuck bumper-to-bumper in their sensible Northern Californian cars.

He stood in an island between waves of traffic and teased the sign gently back and forth. Like a dare on a game at the state fair.

And we were lined up to play.

A sort of cringing panic set in—a feeling that had become all too familiar since I moved there. I had honed the Northern California talent of lamenting the problems that surrounded me but freezing if I confronted them face-to-face. He kept waving the sign; I kept inching forward, closer to the intersection. Waving, inching. Wave, inch.

Suddenly, someone rolled down his window and threw a handful of change at him. He dove down, scrambled in the dust trying to find every coin. The light turned green, and we drove off. He disappeared into a sea of vehicles in my rearview mirror. And I thought, *We've turned everything into a game.*

San Francisco—and the Bay Area in general—has become something of an arcade for the young and plugged in. Uber, Lyft, TaskRabbit, Carbon, Rinse, Instacart, Alfred—a kingdom of cute one-word fiefdoms offering chauffer and butler services for the new tech titans. They are shuttled to their corporate campuses—like summer camp, a world of primary colors and playgrounds and cafés and endless amusement to keep them happy at work. For them, all of life's conveniences can be had at the push of a button; for others, they've got to get running every time the bell rings. The sharing economy meets modern sweat-shop. The gamification of life in the city doesn't mean everyone can afford to play.

Through its history, San Francisco has stood as something like the nation's western capital. But it has always been some-thing of a funhouse mirror, reflecting a strange yet sublime potential self back to the rest of the nation. It bore witness to the Gold Rush, the Transcontinental Railroad, Japanese intern-ment, the Beat poets, the free speech movement, the AIDS crisis and modern LGBTQ politics, and the birth of the semiconductor and motherboard. It was a city of refugees who turned camps into homes—not just the early settlers, but waves of Asian immigrants, families escaping the civil wars in Latin America. It was one of the great centers of America's black middle class, born after World War II as good jobs and free education spelled opportunity for many who saw little of the same in the South. For the past fifty-plus years, San Francisco was a place where community was created, not broken.

After the Great Recession in 2008, while the rest of the coun-try crawled forward, the tech meccas of San Francisco and San Jose sprinted ahead, becoming the two wealthiest cities in the nation. Now the area attracts more educated and wealthy new citizens than ever before. Many believe the region is the engine of a new American economy—a new financial center rivaling those back east—offering much-needed opportunity to the young and brave. If you're thirty and haven't made your mark, you're late to the party.

The problem is that the richer the cities get, the more unequal they get. Specifically, the more young, male, and white they get. And their diversity is being squeezed onto the streets and into distant suburbs by ever-rising rents and living costs. San Francisco's income inequality grew faster than any other American city, making it the most unequal city in the nation in 2015. Salaries in the Bay Area have been on the rise, but the number of people living in poverty has also grown. Now the region is peppered with pairs of twin cities—one rich, one poor, neighboring each other. Compare San Francisco and Oakland, Berkeley and Richmond, Palo Alto and East Palo Alto.

As a result, many of the area's longtime residents are among the first to leave—a worrisome exodus of the very citizens who built these cities. As if radiating from San Francisco and Silicon Valley, economic pressures are pushing whole communities outward. They include rising numbers of veterans, elderly, vulnerable minorities, and others unable to qualify for lucrative jobs in the new tech economy. The current version of San Francisco (2.0, 3.0?) feels deaf to history in favor of a future of its own invention. The different cultures representing the city's past are at risk of being whitewashed away. If you don't have a role to play, there may not be room for you in the Silicon City.

You can feel the pace of change in the city. It has an epidemiology. Quiet blocks in a forgotten neighborhood could have a restaurant, then a few shops, then a condo complex within a year. Busy streets filled with more and more young people in athletic wear, more homeless, and fewer children. (It is a strangely childless city.) Friends moving to the East Bay, to Portland, to the Midwest. Families uprooted not one generation at a time, but in whole genealogies. Sure, San Francisco is changing—and some say it changes all the time—but under stress, cracks in the city's façade are beginning to form.

This project looks into these cracks, through a series of interviews, to document how people are thriving, growing, coping, struggling with the forces transforming the city of San Francisco, Silicon Valley, and the surrounding Bay Area. Part excavation of the forgotten city and part blueprint for what is to come, the book invites us to hear the region speak in chorus: tech innovators, angel investors, social entrepreneurs, political leaders, LGBTQ activists, environmental warriors, recent transplants, old money, homeless youth, kids in schools, poets, pawnbrokers, public defenders, tattoo artists, tour guides, Uber drivers, and union leaders.

I sat with more than 150 people, speaking with many of them for hours: from rural areas to suburbs to cities, across socioeconomic strata and across the lines of gender, race and ethnicity (imagined and constructed as they may sometimes be), native sons and daughters, new residents, and those in and out of the tech industry. Those who participated in this project opened their homes, their thoughts, their feelings to an admittedly lost stranger. For that, I will always be grateful. Our conversations have been transcribed and edited for length and clarity—my voice has largely been removed, and names and identifying details have been changed where prudent—so that these people could speak to readers directly, openly, and honestly.

Each participant tells their story against the backdrop of the region's rapid change, to memorialize the people and values that matter to them, and to mark their place in space and time. No single voice is intended to represent a monolithic feeling of the "community" from which they emerge. These are individuals sharing the world as they—and they alone—see it. Hopefully, they will suggest the silent nuances that remain to be articulated by others whose voices could not be recorded here. These stories are like photographs of a constantly changing kaleidoscope—each turn revealing some truths and admittedly concealing others.

Nevertheless, together they speak to shared experiences: the exodus of the middle class and the poor from the cities; stable structures shaken; the area's unique embrace of and indifference to diversity; tensions between the real and the artificial; loneliness and family; a search for recognition and personal meaning. As if in one voice, they recognize ways in which government and policy seem inadequate and yet never more necessary to address the challenges around them. All, even those who feel they are building the future, beg for a moment to pause, and perhaps pivot. This book offers an opportunity to do both.

These stories speak not just to San Francisco or California, but to America. San Francisco isn't a petri dish sealed off from the rest of the country. It is the product of historical forces and shaped by national and international trends. Wealth inequality is an American problem. The changing workforce, rapid gentrification, infrastructure collapse, climate change, overcrowded prisons, struggling schools, atrophied public institutions—these are problems in any city, in any state across the country. The Bay Area is an experiment in what happens when each of these problems is turned up to 11—what happens when the tech sector fuels changes in the private sector without the public sector being able to keep up—what happens when diversity and disparity combine and combust.

The American Dream shatters—and it has to be rebuilt. We all live in "imagined communities." It's not just the tech community that lives in a bubble. The internet told us we could define the borders of our lives, build our own communities online, drawn for some by our background, our values, our work, our play, our family, our aspirations, our love. And now powerful forces of change have broken many of the happy illusions we had about our communities, cities, neighborhoods, neighbors, even ourselves. It is uncomfortable. Far easier to live in a fantasy world of our own making. America loves the dream but doesn't know how to confront the dream deferred. It explains the panic many of us feel when we are confronted face-to-face with the crises of a diverse society and we cannot step aside or drive away.

But if the people in these interviews offer us new ways of seeing the problem, they also offer solutions. Their stories reveal that presence, physical engagement, and exposure to difference may be the best answer to a transformation that feels alien and lawless. If you want to understand homelessness, go out and meet the homeless; you want to understand students, talk to them; you want to fix a problem, you have to live with it, experience it. This book is maybe the beginning of that process, bringing voices together that live in proximity to one another but are not often part of the same conversation.

The challenge for the Bay Area is not whether it can choose one identity—libertarian tech supercity or state-sponsored liberal utopia—but whether it can find some harmony where the best of each can merge. We can recognize the inherent potential in the Bay Area's current growth, and also wish that the change felt informed and intentional—not incidental and out of control—that it finds ways to make a future that includes San Franciscans new and old alike, where those who built the city can live alongside those who have just arrived. If it cannot happen there, with the wealth of the nation, its brightest talent, and most open hearts at hand, then where will it?

OVERTURE

JOE MASSEY

He picked the restaurant: an old faithful in North Beach, good red sauce, good wine, red leather booths. "There aren't many places like this left," he lamented, tucking a napkin into his collar and ordering a carafe of house red.

came by train. I had so much luggage, but I wanted to see the landscape rather than just floating in a plane. When I left Detroit, there were a couple of feet of snow on the ground. So I watched the seasons change from winter to spring to summer.

I got to Emeryville and took the Amtrak bus over to San Francisco. When we peaked at the top of the Bay Bridge, the suspension section, I looked over at the city, and my only thought was, *I'm home.*

I've been here ever since with no regret. It's an aesthetic feast.

I'd wanted to live in a city that was diverse enough to hold my attention, and there's a lot of diversity here.

San Francisco, it has a great history of jazz. I know Sonny Buxton quite well, real icon, real artist. We used to go to Yoshi's, Yoshi would come out and make an acknowledgment. It is a great pleasure to live in a city that has a respect for local artists—Calvin Keys, one of the greatest guitarists in the world, first seat in the Ray Charles Orchestra; Cal Tjader; Larry Vuckovich, the principal pianist of a real innovator, Lambert, Hendricks & Ross.

I used to sing. *I used to sing!* I had a great voice, baritone, and it's always been easy to get up and jam with anyone. I never pursued it on a professional level, an artistic level, because that demands and commands obedience near to perfection. The difference between mediocrity and genius is measured in patience and commitment.

But I'm a great lover of the art itself. There's no length, except the limit of my pocket, that I wouldn't go to enjoy good music. I enjoy reading, I enjoy travel. I have a kind of curiosity like a butterfly in a flower garden. I'm always happy when I look out, something catches my interest, and I need to learn something new. I want to see it all.

My first real job here was as a tour guide for the Gray Line. I had driven a bus in Detroit, and so converted my license to California. But they weren't hiring anybody to just stand there and talk. The economic mode required you to multitask. I had to drive and speak too. The driving wasn't the hard part. What I had to do, of course, was to find out something about San Francisco.

I felt handicapped not being from this area. So I immersed myself in CDs and history. I started checking out books. After a few months, I realized I started to know a little something. And the more I learned, the more I began to like it. San Francisco has a great story. It grew up at a very crucial time in this country—the end of slavery, end of the Civil War. The Gold Rush. The Big Four—Huntington, Stanford, Crocker, and Hopkins—tycoons who built the western end of the Transcontinental Railroad. On and on.

You know how they got that name, Big Four? The government paid subsidies to any entrepreneur who could build a railroad. And the mileage on flat ground was quite different from mileage in the mountains, because you had to build trellises et cetera. They got, say, $16,000 or $17,000 per mile on flat ground, but $40,000 per mile through the mountains.

Rumor has it, a reporter uncovered a bit of chicanery going on. Turns out they hired a cartographer to "move" the Sierra Mountains some eighty miles further than where they should have been, which of course increased their monies tremendously. The reporter said, "Any four men that can lift up the entire Sierras, those are big people." He coined the name "Big Four." They were like any other big corporation now, completely industrious. Resources came, of course, in the way of gold, as opposed to coal, as opposed to oil.

I think I stayed too long at the party, because I reached a point, on every tour, where I was talking too much. At every corner, I would stop for fifteen minutes. Turns out the layman doesn't care much about history and the discourse is wasted. They can't see the significance—the overall picture of things—how it was, how it used to be. To them, it's all landfill, crazy.

California, thanks to several significant people, has changed the course of history, touched every part of this globe. I've been around this ball of dirt two and a half times, once as a military person, once as a civilian. I've seen the influences of California with my own eyes. It is the melting pot of innovation. What happens in San Francisco, ergo the world.

But I think Steve Jobs's message was completely lost. This era gives us such an opportunity to learn. But instead, the dumbing down of America started many years ago. And our cities, of course, feel it the worst because that's where the population is at its densest.

In its heyday, any Southern black family coming to live in Detroit could live from a single breadwinner—guys that stood on the front lines of the United Automobile Workers and made it possible for the first black kids to go to college. General Motors was the largest employer in the country, three-quarter million. Now Walmart is the largest, with over a million employees, 1.3 or 1.4. They don't make enough money for themselves, let alone to send anybody to college.

Yet here, in San Francisco, kids staring at a screen are making six figures a year and don't have a clue what the world is about. That word, "individual," took the place of a two-syllable word, "person." They use it more and more and more, and I'm trying to figure out why five syllables is better than two.

Years ago, kids were really bright. They knew how to root a tree, save the sap, build a cabin, shoe a horse, save a seed, feed a garden, feed *themselves*. They're perfect idiots now, perfect idiots. Maybe a fucking satellite gets hit by an asteroid. What the fuck are you gonna do now? (Excuse the adjective.)

It is because they are no longer in touch with the source. History is *who we are*. It's not to be discarded. It needs to be studied again and again and again and taught and shared with our lineage. We don't have to get so profound that we overlook the obvious. Technology can't make us forget something as elemental as a baby laughing. Who teaches that baby to laugh?

We need to go back to the Natives—Cherokee, Navajo, Iroquois—they were here before Columbus arrived. The Ohlone people here knew how to do controlled burning, they did it for thousands of years. Archaeological digs on the Ohlone shell mounds show that they lived in relative peace with the other fifty-one native peoples in the central portion of California. In an uninterrupted artistic lineage, from the top of the shell mound down almost five stories and forty miles long, the dig told the same story.

Our ancestry has much to teach us. We need to go back. We need to look. If we don't, *lunacy*. Doing the same shit that don't work, over and over and over, doing the dumbest thing with the worst outcome, and then repeating the process over and expecting something new. It will get worse and prove that sound we hear—the fist thumping on our chest, proclaiming we are the top of the feeding order—is a hollow drum.

PART I

THE NEW
GOLD RUSH

The Gold Rush had the Big Four. Silicon Valley has the Traitorous Eight—men who broke away from Shockley Semiconductor Laboratory in the '60s and formed Fairchild Semiconductor. Fairchild eclipsed Shockley and became the soil from which the industry grew, with companies like Intel and Hewlett-Packard tracing their origins back to that early rift. Intel co-founder Gordon Moore predicted that the speed and efficiency of integrated circuits would double each year, accepted wisdom now known as "Moore's Law." So these companies had simple goals: to make the chips smaller, make them faster, make them more powerful, shrink the world inside our devices and expand their reach.

As the industry evolved, commerce fused with the counter-culture in San Francisco. Psychedelics, dreams of free love and world peace, and science fiction gave the industry something it had been missing: spiritual ambition. Suddenly, through technology, engineers saw the future, new ways of connecting the world, sharing information, flattening hierarchy, shrinking not just microchips but the world. It was no longer enough to make calculators or the computers that ran the space program. People like Steve Jobs saw a world with a "hobby" computer in every home. The inventors of the internet imagined virtual libraries holding infinite information immediately accessible to all.

So the action moved online. "Businesses" became "start-ups;" hardware was replaced by software; storefronts became websites. Yes, tech had its stumbles—the dot-com crash in the early 2000s was a shot to the industry's solar plexus—but it never fell. There always seemed a new horizon. Google brought the world "search," Facebook brought "social," and the era of big data began. The iPhone put a computer in every pocket, and the age of the app arrived. And throughout there have been investors eager to fuel the action. It may seem foolish from the outside, but once the Great Recession arrived in 2008, where else in the world were you going to put your money? Venture capitalists turned small ideas, dreamed up in college dorms, into "unicorns" valued over $1 billion.

And now new names ring out: Jobs, Thiel, Musk, Zuckerberg, Kalanick. Some villains, some heroes, some yet to be defined. Some dreaming of connecting the world, of optimism, opportunity, and a new global harmony; some smelling only youth, ambition, and the Darwinian churn of great ideas mixed with money.

REGIS McKENNA

"Pittsburgh was dying." So he came to California. It was the '60s, and he witnessed the semiconductor boom from ground zero—working for a number of companies that launched from the mother ship that was Fairchild Semiconductor. There he started his own marketing and PR firm, serving the giants of the new industry, like Intel, Apple, Microsoft.

His office has the feeling of a library, or an unfinished exhibit chronicling the history of the tech industry. The conference table is covered with containers of small metal sprockets, arranged like unique species of bugs in a natural history museum. A large silicon ingot is suspended in acrylic glass, like a silver missile hanging in the Smithsonian. Stacks of pamphlets and history books fill the shelves, alongside trophies, old devices, trinkets from around the world, and an antique clock. There's art on most of the walls, leaving no room for a large poster of the original Apple II logo, which lies in a corner, next to an Impressionist oil painting.

They grew the ingots. They grew the ingots, and they sliced them. They did everything on the premises. None of this stuff was done by suppliers, because there *were* no suppliers at the time. I watched the ingots come out of molten silicon. I watched them slice them. I watched them build the cameras and cut the patterns on light tables.

All this was done with less than a few hundred people in a room. Everything was under one roof. The line workers, a little assembly group in the back, were hand-doing all these things. From ingot to calculator, all in the same room.

The designer would take a circuit board and lay it out on paper first, sort of sketch it out and draw his electrical diagrams and so forth. And then he would take these different components, pick them out, and lay them on the paper. That would become a circuit card that had some functionality, some performance level. And then they would test the circuit card. Designers were like Renaissance sculptors. They had two or three top-notch technicians who put the boards together and knew the quirks of their design.

You hear about these eccentric people in the Valley, like Jobs or others, but that goes back to the beginning. There were always people like that.

When I worked at National Semiconductor, there was one guy who did the design. He was one of the strangest people you would ever want to meet. He sort of looked like the Wolfman. He had odd, beady eyes, and he kept an ax in his office. He would show up when he wanted to show up. He would sometimes disappear for weeks at a time. He would go to rodeos in Idaho and just disappear. He wasn't sober half the time. He gave a better talk when he was drinking gin than anytime else. And he was a brilliant designer.

His partner never said three words. But he was so clever with his designs that he would put errors into the data sheet so that nobody could copy them.

The semiconductor business was really rough-and-tumble, really hard-nosed. Because Moore's Law was in effect from the first time you put two transistors together. Getting your product designed and increasing performance became a competitive battle. "Doing it first" meant your survival. So these guys had a different mind-set: *Take no prisoners. Get out there. Everybody works. Everybody is productive*. Like warriors.

Companies didn't raise a lot of money. They worked on cash flow. You got your hands in everything, you learned on the job. People today in a similar position, they would be lucky to leave their cubicle in five years.

The PC industry changed everything. When the industry started out, everybody knew each other—we were all contained within, literally, fifty square miles. The PC created an international market. It drove a trillion-dollar marketplace. It offered something that everybody was looking for, they just didn't know it. The computer became a social entity. You went to these conferences and you found people from all over the world, sharing a common conversation.

———————

Today, there is this misnomer about Silicon Valley, that it is a "start-up community." There's about—I'm guessing—thirty thousand companies in Silicon Valley. Every imaginable technology: fundamental technology, software companies, biotech companies, medical companies. And I've worked with all of them. They always liked ads, because—I don't know—there is something macho about an ad. And they think it says more than it does. I always said, "The ad is the last thing you do." I had this little quote, "The more you advertise a bad product, the faster you go out of business."

We represented so many first-time technologies. We repped the first low-powered laser that was under $100, essentially the first scanners for supermarkets. We worked on the first microprocessor, the first solid-state memory, the first personal computer—I could go on and on. People didn't know what these things were. They were creating new categories of activity, new ways of doing work, new forms of productivity. You can't promote something people don't understand.

So, we did things a little different. We couldn't operate like just any ad agency or PR firm. I hired writers, journalists, not admen. And we saw ourselves as translators for the technical community to the broader public. We focused a lot on market education.

My philosophy was—I've said this my whole career—you have to keep moving backwards, backwards into the organization. You can't stay outside. You can't be on the periphery. You have to move inside and drive it from where the original decisions are being made. With management. That's what we did with Intel, with Apple, with all our clients.

When Steve Jobs and Steve Wozniak came into my office, they had Birkenstocks and cutoffs. Steve had a Ho Chi Minh beard and hair down his back. That actually never, ever bothered me, because I had worked with a lot of crazy people in the semiconductor industry.

They were making "hobby" computers. Things people could

tinker with at home. But Steve had this instinct. He wanted to spread out, go well beyond what anyone else had done. He wanted teachers and students. He wanted a computer in every home. Steve had the vision and Wozniak could build it.

Wozniak had an article that he wanted to place in a magazine, *Byte* magazine in fact, and it was a design for this next new product. And I basically said that the article had to be rewritten because it read like he was talking to himself. It was hobbyist talking to hobbyist, and if he wanted to get the schoolteachers, the students, and beyond that, he'd have to write it to make sense to them. Make English out of it.

Wozniak objected and said something like "I'm not going to have any marketing guy rewrite my stuff."

So I said, "Well, there's the door," and I threw them out. I was up to here anyway. [*He holds his hand to his neck.*]

Steve came back. He just kept coming back. He called. He would sit on my doorstep. Steve was relentless. Relentless. We spent a lot of time together. We went for walks. We talked a lot.

The Apple logo, by the way, I sold to him on the kitchen table upstairs—showing him the layouts. His retort was, "Can we print it on metal?" Because even getting paper to hold the register of all those different colors was quite a task. He made sure he saw it printed on metal before he accepted it. That was for the Apple II, so that was the first logo to appear on their products.* His sense of aesthetics, he had that innately. He was much broader than most people think he was, in terms of literature, in terms of art.

He had a sort of melancholy view of this world. He used to call and tell me about these products coming, but he would

---

* Apple's first iconic product—with a housing, monitor, and keyboard—the Apple II was a huge leap forward from the Apple I, which was just a spare circuit board hobbyists could use to build their own computer.

doubt himself—and whether they would work or not. People focus on his being sort of an ogre in the workplace. But his intolerance was, I think, because he anticipated that he had this little window to make an impact.

When Steve died, throughout the world, people put flowers in front of Apple stores. *The Economist* did an article, saying that Apple was going to decline: "We haven't seen anything revolutionary out of them since the iPhone." I happened to know the guy who wrote the article. I had lunch with him, just to kind of educate him. So I laid out all of these on the table . . .

He starts laying out devices: a Sony Walkman, a Sharp organizer, a Palm Pilot V, an early generation BlackBerry, a Motorola Razr (one of the first flip phones), a DoCoMo phone, and a lineage of iPods and iPhones stretching from 2002 to the present.

Now, if you look at this whole thing—and I said this to the journalist—"Is this incremental improvement? Or is it revolutionary?"

We learn; each generation, we build on the last. And so, none of these on its own is really revolutionary. This one's a music player. This one's a phone. This one is both. This one does everything that is done in here, just with an app.

He holds up a set of vials of water with colorful sediment at the bottom.

And today, these are quantum dots. Each of those vials contains about three or four billion quantum dots, suspended in liquid. They are nanotechnology, "nanodots." You can make transistors out of them. You can make medical devices out of them. Right now, those particular quantum dots are used as crystals. Each crystal can be tuned to a different color—you can create light—and through the quantum dots create a dispersion of true RGB color. These are what Samsung is using in all their new TVs. They make that stuff by the ton now.

I went from the first transistor to this vial. And now I'm on the board of that company!

This is how it works. You pursue the technology. That is the driving force. Everybody is pushing that edge, moving the tech, seeing where they can take it. And then that technology moves into our society. They call it "the tipping point." The only problem with the tipping point is you can only see it in the rearview mirror.

HENDRIK DAHLKAMP

He specializes in teaching machines how to see. Born and raised in Germany, he came to California to study computer science and landed a job at Google working on the self-driving car. He left to launch his own start-up out of his apartment in SoMa. The living room is flanked on two sides with floor-to-ceiling windows. You can look out in 180 degrees and see nothing but sky and city, like you are floating above San Francisco. You can see all the way to the highways—which are jammed solid with cars inching their way east to the Bay Bridge and south toward Google, Facebook, and the peninsula.

"*Disruption.*" *It's a good buzzword, right? It sounds great, and people* here love saying it. But it also responds to the optimization function, which I think is exactly right for society. It implies that there is an openness to actively think about how could you improve things, make things more efficient, better in some ways. It also implies some kind of fairness—that you have a meritocracy where the best idea or the best execution of something wins.

As an engineer, I have the luxury to think like a computer and not feel goofy about it—because if I would feel goofy about that, I would feel goofy about myself all the time. We're trained to think in math, to quantify things, to think in terms of systems, to design system mechanics. So we are like the best of computers and the best of humans. We appreciate a good user interface from a bad one—and sunshine and nature and human interactions and whatnot. It's just for work, we are trained to ignore those things.

I've known from a very young age that I wanted to do something with computers. I think I was eight: my uncle had a computer, and he went on a long vacation and left it in the basement. It was 100 percent English, and it had a text-only interface back in the day. That was 1987, and I spent all my free time in front of it. I had no idea what any of the words meant on the screen, but, when I typed this, then something happened. I managed to write a very short program, to play around with the word processor, print a letter. I was always trying to figure out how to get new things from it, because I wanted to see it all.

Then, when I was twelve, Christmas, I got my own, a Commodore Amiga 500, and spent a lot of time in front of it. My parents put a time limit on it. I only had an hour a day, but that made it even more interesting to squeeze the most out of it.

I arrived here in September of 2004 to get my PhD, and by October, I was in the Mojave Desert. The research group I joined had started a really cool project, building a car that drives itself.

There was a race called the DARPA Grand Challenge, 150 miles, autonomous cars racing through the desert.*

I built the computer vision: using a combination of lasers and cameras to figure out what the road looks like and to decide when we could drive faster and slower. In the desert, you just had to drive straight ahead, but on real roads, you had to look all around you for other cars, for lane markers and so on.

So we decided to just play with it. We drove every single street of Palo Alto. The sensors recorded everything. We put all of that data on a map: you could just click on any point and you saw the panorama of the street. The tech wasn't all that complicated, but it made for a pretty cool demo because you click on any address and get immersed. You could hit a button and travel along the road.

Larry Page, the CEO of Google, he loves self-driving cars. He's a big alpha geek in technology. He actually came to the DARPA Grand Challenge. Half my team joined Google and quickly built up a fleet of these cars, not just one. We had a hundred cars in the country and four hundred worldwide. We turned the mapping function into a product that became Google Street View.

The vision always was to have cars take over driving—that you don't have to worry about it at all. You can sit in the back and relax and read or get on with your life. You get your car to drive you from A to B and then the car does something else: picks up your kids or gets rented out or whatever.

It would truly disrupt how our society works. It can reduce traffic congestion. You look at the highway, if you take a picture,

* The Defense Advanced Research Projects Agency (DARPA) invests on behalf of the US government in groundbreaking technology for national security. It hosted a series of competitions, challenging students from the nation's top universities to demonstrate breakthroughs in robotics and autonomous vehicles.

I think 92 percent of it is empty and only 8 percent is filled by cars, because humans are bad drivers and need all this safety distance between them. With a self-driving car, you could drive much more efficiently, faster and closer together with a lower accident rate. You don't need parking. Look out of the window, a big part of the city is parking lots. You waste all this real estate in the best locations storing stuff that rusts. You can change urban architecture. It allows elderly people to participate in life because, when they can't drive anymore, they get cut off from their friends.

So, that vision for self-driving cars is great, but the part that's really hard and, honestly, isn't solved yet by any of the players, is to make it really robust and reliable. The big metric there is miles per incident: how many miles do you drive before there is an incident? This number is surprisingly good for human driving. There is an accident, like a fender bender, if I read the statistics correctly, every 165,000 miles driven. That is a really high bar for a self-driving car to clear—because you would only trust the system if it is better than a human. I actually left the project because it didn't happen quickly enough for me.

So I founded a start-up. Start-ups are a creative and very impactful way in which you can build something cool efficiently and quickly. The speed and the creativity in which they can execute, just do things without a hundred meetings.

All I want to do is build beautiful things—systems that work beautifully, that are very nicely engineered, efficient, that don't waste resources, and that do something better than it was done before: cool systems that bring us further as a society, that help do something in the real world.

COCO CONN

She has a sprightly way about her. As if everything can be discovered again for the first time. An artist who wandered the world, she stumbled into San Francisco in the 1970s and made it her home. She was part of an early community of counterculture figures, futurists, and psychedelics who revolutionized Bay Area culture and transformed the tech industry. They moved it beyond calculators, scientific instruments, and aerospace and gave it purpose, vision, and global (perhaps galactic) scope. In short, they injected technology with a sense of inspiration and values, with its own religion. Today, Coco is an artist and educator who continues to preach the gospel of those early days.

San Francisco seemed to have a different spirit. It seemed wilder and more courageous than L.A. They had talent, but we had irreverence—which is more important, right?

It was a very heady time. So many new ideas. And everyone was sharing and comparing. I remember seeing the first black letters on a white screen—the fact that the screen wasn't green—it was like, "Whoa, you can do that?" People were developing a new language, so every new word was so exciting. Some of the best ideas in science fiction, whether it was *True Names* or books from the early 1900s, became explosive. And of course there was everything happening in the culture, in politics and technology—the space program. Technology was somehow going to bring us together and allow us a chance to talk, so we can work things out instead of kill each other. All these simplistic ideas drove that mad rush. It was like being in the eye of a hurricane: you can't feel the impact.

I fell into a large group at the Burning Man. They were on fire—their abandon. I just fell madly in love. And I became famous for collecting crazy nerds. The wackier, the better.

John Draper, "Captain Crunch," he'd whistle and simulate these phone signals. He could stand in a phone booth and whistle his way through all these phone systems, go loop the world, and then call the phone booth next to him. He was frequency, sound, modulation.

The Shulgins, Anna and Sasha. Molecule by molecule, these two people tried out hundreds of combinations of drugs that never got released. "Sasha makes something new, we try it, we go to bed, we make love. In the morning, we have a big bowl of soup and talk about it." But you go to Brazil, and an Indian in a jungle is having similar visions. Drinking ayahuasca is like plugging into the umbilical cord of the planet. Realms that we don't know how to navigate until people experiment, try.

John Perry Barlow. He was such a cowboy—so cool and fun—you couldn't resist that. He founded the Electronic Frontier Foundation, with John Gilmore and Mitch Kapor, because he didn't want the government to run away with this new technology. He thought technology should be free. He was never afraid of speaking the truth or confronting "givens."

We would throw parties and bring these incredible people together: filmmakers, computer graphics people, politicians, musicians, hackers. People you wouldn't otherwise meet in your life, people you'd never see together in the same place if it weren't for him. He was an amazing bridge between cultures. And the psychedelic side was really important to John. People need to be awakened. They need that chaos factor.

Tim Leary would come. I would drag him off to events, and we'd sing in the car and laugh. His exuberance for wanting to adapt technology was so infectious. He loved technology. I think he genuinely knew that there was something thrilling, something new. He wanted to be part of it, and he wanted to know all about it.

I called him one day, I said, "Tim, my friend has a machine, and you put little sensors on your temples and it measures your alpha, beta, theta levels of your brain, and you can control what's on the screen."

He goes, "I wanna try it."

So I ran, picked him up, brought him to my house, and he spent quite some time with playing with what we could make show up on the screen. My friend looked at me and said, "I've shown this to a lot of people. Tim has really more control over the levels of his brain than anybody I've ever seen."

They were a wild group of people. People with talent. People who knew that the simplest solutions could solve the biggest problems. That there was collective wisdom, ancient cultures, primordial connections, music, so much to learn from. They knew that money doesn't drive everything.

TIM DRAPER

The office of his venture capital firm is one block from El Camino Real—the road that used to connect the Missions during the Spanish colonization of California and now snakes down the tech corridor from San Francisco to San Jose. The walls are covered with huge murals of superheroes—Batman, Superman, Wonder Woman—frozen in action poses.

My grandfather was the first venture capitalist in Silicon Valley. My dad moved here, joined him, and became one of the pioneers of the business. So I grew up here when El Camino was a dirt road. Downtown Menlo Park had about five stores total.

I've watched this whole metropolis build around Silicon Valley, and tried to get to the heart of what makes this ecosystem work. I've been the Johnny Appleseed of venture capital—spreading the seeds of this valley everywhere I go. You need angel investors who work together to fund start-ups. You need one big company from your region, some entrepreneur that's built something, and you got to promote the heck out of that. You need a good technical university nearby, maybe a good business school too. You need a series of events where great entrepreneurs come and speak and everybody else gathers, because it's inspirational for everybody else. You need the lawyers to simplify the system so it just moves like a machine. Then you need the press to start writing about these companies as though they are heroes.

Exporting this vision wasn't easy—you really had to sort of be a pioneer with arrows on your back. New York, L.A., Pittsburgh, Chicago, Utah, Denver, Alaska. Each new place, we had to fight it out with some lawyer. Or the press didn't really want to write about it. Or the bankers, accountants, headhunters, they weren't in the ecosystem yet, so we needed to gather them together. Normally, we'd hold a big event, bring them all together, make sure they were all talking to each other, and let them know that we were in business.

We were even the first Silicon Valley firm to invest internationally. It felt like we were going into the Great Beyond. Might as well have been going to Mars.

I went to China, and I remember talking to the minister of economics. He said, "You must invest in our country."

I said, "Why should I? There's a guy that I ran into that built a $90 million chocolate company here, and you nationalized it. You took it from him."

He said, "What would you suggest?"

I said, "Well, you've got to make sure that anyone that does invest early makes *a lot of money*, so they can go tell their friends. Then they'll all come, they'll all invest in China."

We invested in a bunch of Chinese businesses, sharing with them the insights of all of these interesting US companies they could learn from: Badoo, a search engine; Focus Media is like their Clear Channel; and ePay, their PayPal.

Companies have a natural life. They have a natural way of growing, and if you mess with that too much, it changes everything. If an entrepreneur gets too much money, they feel like they can spend their way out of all of their problems, instead of getting creative. Businesses have to ride a few waves. They have to be built through cycles, endless cycles. They have to figure out the model, know who their customers are, and know that if they put in a dollar they get out five. When that happens, it's time to raise a lot of money.

It's instinctive for me. You have to see what it is in the entrepreneur that *matters*, and you have to see what's going on in technology that *matters*. We meet with young entrepreneurs, it's all about their enthusiasm. Because that's the kind of thing that will take them through the whole process. It's something they can't fake. You ask them why they are doing it, it spills out—"It's so exciting, all of those other people are doing it wrong, we've got a great avenue, and we know exactly what we're going to do!" If they say they're doing it for the money, that's not enough, because money will just come and go, come and go.

I've seen start-ups change an industry and challenge huge companies. We saw Tesla change the auto industry, Skype changed the long-distance carriers, and Hotmail changed the post office. Huge things are happening out there, over the last forty-five to fifty years. So much improvement, thanks to the private sector.

I always describe these entrepreneurs as heroes. Heroes are our past, the people we look back on and say they did great things. But superheroes are our future—whether they are industrialists, leaders of societies, or revolutionaries. They are focused on the future. We need to find some superheroes.

COLIN RULE

He grew up in Amarillo, Texas, and studied conflict resolution in Boston. Silicon Valley was the farthest place from where he thought he'd end up. He is a Quaker, and has the affable optimism of someone who believes consensus can be reached with anyone, anywhere: "We all have a little God inside of us, and if my little part of God and your little part of God can see each other, we can work it out." He spent the first half of his career working on peace-building projects around the world. Then, suddenly, he was recruited by eBay, relocated west, and his whole life changed. He is now the CEO of a leading dispute-resolution company in tech. He works with major corporations and local governments alike. We met after he gave a talk about moving the American court system online.

e*Bay was a very hot company. It was kind of like the Facebook of the time.* So they flew me out here. I was going to consult for four or five days.

I was just wide-eyed about Silicon Valley! They talked about "Nerdvana"! I did my four or five days, answered questions best I could, gave them an invoice, and then flew home. I thought, *Wow, that was pretty cool. That was fun.*

About a month later they called me. They were asking interview questions, "People like you, and they think that you know what we need to know." They made me an offer. I looked at it, and I was like, *I guess I work for eBay now.*

They just came on strong. "We're going to move you out here. We're going to set you up with a Realtor." They wanted me out immediately, and then my family could follow a month later. Very whirlwind. I know a lot of people that this has happened to. When they say they want you, how can you not?

I was a more senior person. But I have seen people that get pulled straight out of school, young people. They get an apartment right next to the campus. There's posters for a movie tonight at nine p.m. The restaurants are open for breakfast, lunch, and dinner. Really their whole life, their whole sense of identity becomes intertwined with the company.

Rapid wealth to people in their youth can be profoundly disorienting. Silicon Valley, you're almost like a lottery winner. It happens so fortuitously and quickly that you can't really interpret it. And then a lot of people impose their narratives upon you. You become obsessed with replicating it to prove that it wasn't a fluke.

Some people get very, very panicky and emotional. It doesn't have to be massive success, Zuckerberg success. But still they feel like, *Look, I came here, and I started this company. I made a lot of money. So clearly the way I see the world is the correct way to see the world.* Some of them, in reaction, become very . . . aggressive about it.

And that was shocking to me, as someone who had done the Peace Corps in Africa, just the myopia of some of the people here. I wanted to shake some of those people up, or at least grab them by the collars and say, "Really?"

eBay had what we called the leaky bathtub. When I first showed up, there were so many buyers pouring into the bathtub, it was just growing, growing, growing. They were expanding to new countries. But the drain was bad: they were losing people who had bad experiences.

When somebody has a bad experience, they leave and you never hear about it. They don't tell you. You can email them all you want. They are gone. They are never going to come back, and that's terrifying to these MBAs. They pay a lot of money to acquire these customers.

For me, resolving a dispute was a self-evident good. But for them it was, like, "Let's just pay them all off."

What I proved with the numbers was, if somebody has a problem and you address that problem—even if they don't win, regardless of outcome—they are much more loyal to you than the people that never had a dispute in the first place. And we pulled it off. We did 60 million disputes a year, and I was there for eight years. That's hundreds and hundreds of millions of resolutions.

There were 250 million users at eBay, and there were lots of different kinds of disputes. Sometimes the bidder would win, but they wouldn't pay. Sometimes a thirteen-year-old bids a million dollars on a Ferrari, and the seller goes, "Great, a million dollars," but there's no way that kid is ever going to pay.

We had reputation disputes, slander-libel type of disputes. We had intellectual-property disputes where somebody would list an item and somebody else would come and steal their description and steal their photos and then list another item, saying, "Oh, I have that item too."

Somebody in China would start to sell knock-off drills that were black and yellow. Sometimes they would say they are Black & Decker, obviously that's a clear violation. But other times they would say "cordless drill" in the same typeface. We called those "verified rights owner disputes."

Somebody was selling used underwear. "I'm the homecoming king" or "I'm captain of the football team and I wore this underwear when we won the big game," and the underwear would sell for $350.

We had someone who sold communion wafers that they got from Pope John Paul in St. Peter's. They got in line, took communion, and pocketed the wafers. They kept them for six, seven years. Then Pope John Paul passed away, and they put these wafers on eBay. Obviously, for Catholics, that's huge. Once the wafers are blessed, that is the flesh of Christ. So if you take it, you have to eat it. Pocketing it is sacrilege.

We had another one where somebody was selling a bathtub. It was the bathtub that the guy who killed Martin Luther King stood on in the motel room to shoot. We heard that and said, "Take it down. Immediately take it down. That's offensive. That's a hate object." It turns out the National Civil Rights Museum was selling it. Somebody had donated that bathtub to them, but they were going to sell it to get money to fund the museum. Now, we had to decide. You can't set a policy for items based on who is selling it: *If the Klan is selling the bathtub, that's wrong. If the National Civil Rights Museum is selling the bathtub, that's okay.* That's not a policy that works.

We essentially had to build a civil justice system. A lot of people at eBay were these young guys, they start these websites in their twenties, and they are total libertarians. "I'm not going to censor anybody. Everybody can say whatever they want." Obviously, if you're a teenager, you're like, "These old people with their rules! I'm going to create a total open marketplace of ideas." Then, you see the practical effect of this. And you start to build some rules.

But it turns out, eBay was a *time*. The internet was new and nobody knew how to buy anything. Macy's wasn't online. Walmart wasn't online. So eBay solved that problem. You could go to eBay, type in some weird thing, and it would come up.

People ask, "What killed eBay?" All these stores got online, Amazon scaled, and Google killed eBay. Now, if you want to go buy a Beanie Baby, you go to Google and you type in Beanie Baby and there are fifty places to buy it.

Google is a *time*, and Google has done a good job of reinventing itself to stay relevant. Facebook has done the same thing. But think about AOL, CompuServe, Friendster . . . Who knows, something new can always come up. It's creative destruction. It's Schumpeter.* That's what the Valley is all about. Go invent the next thing. Disrupt.

When I started my company in Boston, it was so hard. There's a cultural conservatism in the Northeast. Funders are like, "I don't really get it. Why don't you go prove that you're a sure thing and then come back to me?"

Whereas Silicon Valley, culturally—and I think this is the old hippie, DIY thing—it's about what's new. *Do you have passion? Has the world not seen this before? Great. Let's do it. Let's get some money and let's give it a shot.* That passion exists so much that they fund really stupid ideas. *What's new? What's next? What's coming?*

The culture out here *encourages* you to fail. People think, *Well, you learned something. You tried to do what was next. You got it wrong, but that's a plus.* Throw a lot of stuff out there. A lot of it is going to fail. You just have to keep throwing stuff, throwing stuff, throwing stuff, throwing stuff. That's American optimism. Everybody wants a chance. But there's a lot of misery that comes from that lottery system.

These instincts exist in Amarillo, Texas. It's just they are starting muffler stores. They start a Subway franchise. You can't get millions and millions of dollars. You can't start a big internet

* Economist Joseph Schumpeter described "creative destruction" as a kind of mutagenic or Darwinian force at the heart of capitalism—one that "incessantly revolutionizes the economic structure from within, incessantly destroying the old one, incessantly creating a new one."

company. They're not playing in the same league. And I don't think that the culture necessarily embraces the new.

Every place has its own mythology. We lionize these heroes, like Steve Jobs. "It will rain tomorrow," he says. And then it rains, we say, "Oh, you're a genius!" Either the rain is going to come or the rain is not going to come. But if you can call it right, people will believe in magic.

LISA CHU

We are sitting in the UC Berkeley quad on a bench in the shade of a large tree. This is practically her hometown. She points to where she grew up, where her siblings lived and studied, and where she lives on campus now. We can hear a group gathering across campus to protest the invitation of a right-wing pundit. The university was the cradle of the 1960s free-speech movement and remains something of a center of progressive politics. Today, the school also acts as a pipeline to careers in tech, tempting students with all the industry promises.

The Berkeley Computer Science Department has a ratio like 1:6 or 1:9 females to males. My first day, I walked in—it's a class of, like, thirty people, you could count the women on one hand—and I was, *Ugh, this is going to be a great semester. . . .*

I'm Asian, I'm female, I'm of small stature, I take hard classes, right? But I really, really, really hate being lumped into the quiet-Asian-small-girl stereotype.

I play the tuba, I started in high school. People were like,

"The instrument is bigger than you are!" And that kind of got to: "Fuck you, I'm going to play this instrument, and I'm going to play it damn well!" It became part of a newfound self awareness and independence. I got rebellious a little bit.

I don't know if I can apply the same spirit to CS. People keep telling me that computer science is all about perseverance and grit. Even if you're not gunning to be the next Bill Gates, whatever, as long as you work hard you'll be fine. But I do think there's a certain way you have to think about computer-science stuff—a certain way you need to approach problems. And I don't know that I've developed that sense. So I'm worried I'm going to keep pushing all this energy into CS, and it's not going to be enough. It all really boils down to fear.

But then, every day at UC Berkeley, college life gets everyone riled up. Whenever there's a protest that gains momentum, all the other causes kind of tack onto it. A protest on fee hikes becomes a protest on fracking, becomes a protest on racial inequality, becomes Occupy, becomes Muslim rights, becomes fuck UCPD.

It makes you aware. Inspired. Maybe it's the West Coast. The Bay Area has a . . . dynamism. People recycle here. People care more. If you see something wrong, you can have an impact. Ideals. It feels like there's this movement towards change.

That's part of why I'm comfortable with computer science. It's because of technology that we're able to connect with all these different people in various parts of the world instantaneously and suddenly be able to think on a more global level. So computers and making an impact are inherently intertwined.

If it was solely up to me, I think I would rather do the agent-of-change thing. But there is such pressure on campus, and in the area, to join tech. I would feel a little bit guilty if I went off and did my own thing and (not really) threw away all that my dad, my parents, worked for. My mom passed away at the beginning of my sophomore year in high school. Cancer. My dad really, really wanted me to go here, to have that bragging right—for me to study computer science, *nudge, nudge, nudge*—to give his daughter a good future.

Then again, my mom was a lot like me, I've been told. We're both feisty. We both have bad tempers. We're both a little rebellious.

She wrote a lot, she did photography. We have a bunch of photos hanging in my house, she took all of them. She made my clothes, she would make me all these dresses when I was growing up. Once I hit middle school, suddenly it was not cool to wear dresses to school, and I would be like, "No one else wears dresses in school."

And she'd be like, "Why are you trying to go off of what other people are doing? You need to be independent." I learned, *Okay, just wear it like you like it, and no one else cares.*

She had really big dreams, and those got stalled a lot after she got diagnosed. And when all the side effects came in—loss of hearing and her not being able to speak English . . . She really wanted to come to America and go into law—or do something really grand—and it all just kind of got stalled. . . . She ended up staying at home and taking care of me and my sister. And she devoted her efforts to us.

My mom would want me to go to law school. If everything was an ideal world, I would double major in CS and something else. I would work at some badass nonprofit, travel and do all this cool stuff, also make money so I can pay off all my college bills. And then once I'm stable and I've traveled and I've done all the hands-on change stuff that I want to do—then I would go to law school, become a judge or a lawyer, and then do political work.

Going to Berkeley and being surrounded by all these brilliant people, you realize how ordinary your intelligence is. There's this feeling of having to prove yourself. You have to carve out your own identity. I think I have the balls to do that.

CHARLES CARTER

He started his career in urban planning, working for the cities in the East Bay. First Emeryville, a small city parked between Berkeley and Oakland. Then Richmond, a once-thriving industrial city to the north. A talented young planner, he thought he could spend his career helping the Bay Area "transition from true industry, converting factories and shipyards to creative incubation spaces." Then, Stanford made him an offer he could not refuse, and he moved his family to Palo Alto. He spent a nearly thirty-year career in its Office of Land, Buildings and Real Estate, overseeing the infrastructure and physical development of the campus.

I lived through the greatest-ever growth period at Stanford. When I came in '82, we would be doing one major building at a time. We never had five, six major buildings going on simultaneously, like we did when I left. Now it looks like it will stay like that as long as the university can afford it.

Stanford probably operates more like a business than any other university. Its success has always been tied to the land endowment, and that land endowment has also enabled its business success. The research park, the shopping center. We used to get these field trips from other universities who'd say, "Well, we got this excess land, and we understand you made some money off of yours. So could you maybe show us how to do that?"

Stanford is 8,400 acres across six different jurisdictions. The campus is about 2,200 acres. That's including the medical center. Take another 2,000 acres for Jasper Ridge Biological Preserve. Then a couple thousand other acres that are developed commercially, the shopping center. Even everything on the far side of Page Mill, between Foothill and El Camino, all the way over to the VA Hospital, that's all Stanford land. All those tech companies in there, all those law firms in there, Stanford is their landlord.

Something like half the jobs in Palo Alto are on Stanford land. The daytime population is something like 60 percent higher than the residential population. It's a job center. So Stanford is not just driving economic development by creating ideas and innovation. It's providing the bricks and mortar where this stuff occurs. It has not only fostered the relationship between academics and the people selling ideas, it makes money on the ideas itself. You get bigger by getting bigger, by feeding the beast.

That starts to get real murky, because it's a private institution. The whole Hennessy-Google thing. John Hennessy was the president of Stanford University. The guys that started Google, they were students of his. Now he's a shareholder, and he sits on the board. In fact, he's maybe the most powerful person on the Google board. So there's a lot of entanglement when you start to dig around.

In my department, priorities would change depending upon the wealth and influence of the donor paying for the project or the makeup of the board at the time. Decisions being made at a very high level. This donor and this board member would call my boss, and the next thing I knew we were building a new business school. Even efforts to push the humanities along have been guided in a specific direction by a specific donor—not the outgrowth of a holistic education policy or vision for the university.

I don't think Stanford's necessarily lost its higher calling. I think the academicians still believe they're doing useful things. But I've definitely heard it called the world's most successful technical college. We had an intern who used to love to wear this T-shirt that said something like GO TO STANFORD. HAVE BIG IDEAS. MAKE LOTS OF MONEY. *Ah, so there needs to be a practical end to this great thinking you're doing.*

Have you ever read the original founding document? It says all kinds of things—they pick and choose what to use, like the

Bible. It says that all the lands, thus given and endowed, are to be used henceforth and evermore for the advancement of the university.* Now, that's liberally interpreted—that's why Stanford land is never sold.

It talks about practical education—I can't remember the exact language—but the founders wanted people to do useful things.† So the *pure learning*, knowledge for knowledge's sake—which we all understood college to be at some point—they dispensed with that early on at a policy level. It ain't the "Farm" anymore. Some of it is just raw ambition. The Gold Rush ain't about nothing but getting rich, right?

CAILLE MILLNER

An author and columnist for the *San Francisco Chronicle* who grew up in the Bay Area, she has followed the tech industry as it spread from San Jose to San Francisco, uncovering many stories along the way. "It's good to be here as a writer because no one is paying attention, no one reads here, so there is freedom to it. It's a powerful position—I can watch, I can observe."

---

* The Stanford University Founding Grant provides that the gifted land "shall constitute the foundation and endowment for the University herein provided, and upon the trust that the principal thereof shall forever remain intact, and that the rents, issues, and profits thereof shall be devoted to the foundation and maintenance of the University hereby founded and endowed, and to the uses and purposes herein mentioned."

† The Founding Grant intends that "the instruction offered must be such as will qualify the students for personal success and direct usefulness in life."

W*hen we were growing up, there were still farms. There were still* orchards and the people who lived there. It's curious, because I think it somehow explains the politics.

We lived in a very, very racially diverse, economically diverse neighborhood. There were a lot of educated black people who were in the tech industry, believe it or not. Or, like my dad, they were professionals or academics. My brother and I grew up with Mexicans and Filipinos, part of a pack of kids just roaming the streets. I think that's still my platonic ideal.

In the '80s, there was IBM. That was it. You went there. You worked there for your entire career. You were making the equivalent of planes or heavy equipment—technology for businesses and not consumers. It was a very solid, middle-class, white-collar place, not completely out of scale or out of order with anything else that was going on in the rest of the country.

In the '90s, that changed. The first wave of consumer-driven technology companies hit, and the money really started coming in.

Growing up here, looking at it from the outside, I'm not sure that anyone believed it was gonna last. People didn't realize. They thought, *IBM will always be around. It will always be there if this little company doesn't work out.* The stakes didn't feel as high as they do now.

The people who moved out here, they were coming from Texas, Oklahoma, Kansas. They were all white males, and they didn't necessarily have fancy educations. And they were also kind of weird. These were very strange people, very socially maladjusted. They had grown up with computers, they did it from childhood. And they had very serious beliefs about it.

Technology was how they connected to the world. They talked about it having this Messiah-like reality: *Technology is free and has the power to connect us all.* You see it in those early chat rooms, projects like Wikipedia and Craigslist, the guys who created Netscape. Those were Tech 1.0. A lot of those guys weren't in it for the money. They were in it because that was how they saw the world. They were just too utopian, really.

We're just gonna do some weird, free-wheeling stuff. We're gonna start this weird company and call it Yahoo! We're gonna have "surfers" who are gonna look through the net and order things like librarians. No one took it seriously. No one thought like, *Oh, this is going to become a serious business.* No one thought this little company was going to become an institution.

Eventually they paved over all of the farm country and all the orchards. They put up housing, built very few businesses. And the area got bleaker. My parents were making more money. And we moved to the "better" part of town. It was so sterile. No children, no one to play with.

When the jobs went away, the working class just simply becomes "not working." Now there are very few black people in the South Bay. The Mexicans who worked good jobs in construction, farming, they have become the underclass. And San Jose became this weird core of Middle America in California—people from Dust Bowl geography with Dust Bowl mentality—surrounded by educated people of color.

"Normal" people did not start getting into tech until 2.0. People talk about the "tech bros," but they wouldn't have had anything to do with the first tech boom. They understand tech as a business, *We wanna grow. We want to make X amount of dollars. We wanna scale. We wanna do this, we wanna do that.*

They are billionaires wearing hoodies.

My parents came when they were children, and there was opportunity here. None of their parents had been here but they all knew something small, very small, about California that led them to think this was where their kids could do something with their lives. They thought, even black people could get educated here. They could get higher education—the college and the state university system was free. My parents were at Berkeley in the '60s, the student movement and all of the unrest. My dad went to all the marches and all the rallies.

As a result of specific policy changes, political changes, and social changes, California is now a climate of restriction and not-having and scrambling, as opposed to a place where you can make something of yourself. Kids in California now are faced with fences as opposed to the open plain.

My dad said something back when the changes started. He was like, "Oh, there are too many Mexicans. There are too many Asians here. Watch what happens. As soon as they all go into the school system, they're going to stop putting money into the schools."

Prop 13 is what happened.* The tax backlash was enormous. We also had a very serious situation with the criminal justice system; we incarcerated a lot of people here. So we defunded the schools, and we funded the prisons. Those two things are directly based on demographic change. People of color, we've been dealing with this forever.

California, it feels like we've given up on big policy changes. We've given up on trying to do big solutions and ceded that ground to the business of tech. I don't know how well that's going to work out.

We natives, those of us who grew up here, the question of our lives is *When is the bust coming?* Because there have been so many. People joke, "We're gonna wait for the bust, and then we can go to that restaurant again." It applies to larger things

---

* A 1978 ballot initiative that cut property taxes and capped their increase. The measure drained local school districts of a critical source of funds and disproportionately affected large cities, where schools suffered most.

too—because it's only then, in these little windows, when the money isn't crazy, you can actually buy a house, have a kid, do these things that normal adult people do. So you wait for the bust to make progress in your life. To have some space.

And so we always say, *But there will be a bust, but there will be a bust, but there will be a bust* . . .

PART II

THE SOUL OF
THE CITY

There's the Financial District and industrial SoMa to the east. To the north, up Russian Hill, through Pacific Heights (or "Pac Heights"), to the Marina, wider streets, larger houses, traditionally wealthier areas. In between, there's Chinatown and North Beach, full of cafés and old Italian restaurants. To the south, the Castro, the Mission, Bernal Heights. To the west, the Western Addition, the Richmond, the Sunset. In the middle, the Fillmore and the Tenderloin. The names of many of these neighborhoods have been shaped by the early history of the city. The Mission was the site of the early Spanish mission; Bernal Heights and Noe Valley were named after family farmsteads and early land grants ceded to the city; Russian Hill was named after a small Russian cemetery discovered there by Gold Rush settlers.

And the great upheavals of the twentieth century that gave the neighborhoods their modern character. North Beach became the home of the Beats, the City Lights bookstore their shrine. The Castro and the Mission, once predominantly Irish neighborhoods, received wave after wave of Latin American immigrants escaping revolution and unrest to the south; these areas later became home to gay and lesbian communities. The western neighborhoods drew an eclectic mix of hippies, Asian, Russian, and African communities, each carving space while integrating into what came before. A black middle class, one of the few in America, drawn after World War II by jobs in shipping and the factories lining the bay, made its home in the Fillmore. Then, when the ports slowed and shipyards like Hunters Point were decommissioned, housing projects like the Bayview grew in their place.

This historical archaeology was preserved for decades, giving many the hope that the cultural map of San Francisco might be carved in its bones. The city grew richer, the city grew poorer, neighborhoods grew more colorful; the city made space for those who arrived. It had a way of absorbing the friction. Recent years have tested that tradition. The tech boom drew a new wave of settlers seeking gold and the chance to be part of building the future. As many as ten thousand new residents arrived in some years, many of them well credentialed, well paid, and far too young to settle down in the suburbs nearby.

And San Francisco ran out of space. In the battle for housing, new won over old. Evictions spiked—leases broken, nuisance claims issued, illegal roommates, obscure legal provisions invoked. More than five thousand evictions since 2010 clustered in working-class neighborhoods like the Mission, the Tenderloin, and the Western Addition. Longtime residents moved as far as Antioch, to Gilroy, to Stockton, commuting sometimes two hours to hold on to the job they had worked their whole lives in San Francisco.

New residents came in such numbers that they spread across the city, terraforming the ecosystem to suit their appetites and threatening to trample the relics of lives that once inhabited the same space. The comforts of life as a hipster techie slowly replaced the individual character of the communities that once defined the city.

SAMI RAHUL

We drive through the Marina in his truck. He points out his favorite buildings as we pass. He grew up in Sacramento and moved here as soon as he could afford it: "San Francisco opens you up. It puts you on the front lines of innovation. I felt that energy here. I felt like I can be a part of something bigger, that connection to the possibilities." He got a job selling cable door-to-door.

Mind you, I'm still learning the city, the neighborhoods. They give you a lead sheet with a bunch of addresses. People who have cable or people who don't.

My first territory was Pac Heights. And I didn't know shit about Pac Heights. I drove out, parked my truck, and started knocking on doors. I quickly noticed, *These homes are freaking amazing. These are mansions, mini mansions.* But that didn't deter me. I started knocking on these doors, and I quickly noticed a lot of help was answering—butlers and maids—and I was tripping out. Every once in a while, I stopped and looked at these beautiful views.

One of the names on the list was Jessica McClintock, and that name stuck out to me. I'm like, *Jessica McClintock? Where have I heard that name?* She's a wedding-dress designer, a *famous* wedding dress designer. My wife wanted a Jessica McClintock dress for our wedding.

They have all these little pitches that they teach you—like how you can save money if you add phone service with us. I'm trying to pitch this to Jessica McClintock's butler, but I'm like, *What the hell am I doing? I'm trying to save these billionaires sixteen bucks a month by adding phone service.* I got no sales out of Pac Heights. None.

But an old salesman—he was from New York, a classic, strong Brooklyn personality—he schooled me in the game. He took me out to a couple of housing projects. As a child, I had grown up in public housing, but I didn't think that's where you got sales. *Go where the money's at,* right? But these housing projects—near the Fillmore area, even some down in Sunnydale—if you knocked on doors, people were home. Some of them had $500 cable bills a month. Those were the gold mines. The first day, I got ten sales.

I'm still not a good salesman. I get lost in conversations, and I don't see the end of the deal. But I've learned a lot: in my truck, driving around, knocking on doors, seeing the beautiful architecture and learning those neighborhoods. Or, on foot, seeing different, almost hidden gems. Meeting different people. Understanding the city.

Understanding that in some respects, you turn a block here in San Francisco, you're in a different little world.

PAUL GILLESPIE

In his rent-controlled apartment looking over Dolores Park, he has a mattress, sheets, a table, some chairs, and a small shelf with

books and records, analog only. Outside, through a broken win-
dowpane, San Francisco's young bask shoulder to shoulder in the
early spring sun. Through all the bodies, you can barely see the
green of the lawn. He has driven a cab in San Francisco for nearly
forty years.

California has always attracted get-rich-quick artists. Starting from
the Gold Rush, people come to make a lot of money and
leave. Gary Snyder, the poet, once said, "The most radical thing
you can do is stay home." Find somewhere to stay put, and really
get to be a part of a place, to understand it. Not flit around,
exploiting as you go.

I hear kids talking about how they are going to "solve the
money problem." They are going to make a lot, a whole lifetime's worth of money, and then just kick back. Like Napster
and Facebook and everyone that got very, very wealthy, very,
very young.

San Francisco used to attract the offbeat, the bohemian, the
one who is different, the one who didn't come here to make
money. If you want to make money, you went to New York. If
you wanted to become famous, you went to Los Angeles. The
people who came to San Francisco were just as smart, maybe
smarter, but they didn't really care that much about money.
They cared about being themselves and finding people who
were a little offbeat too.

I hitchhiked out here from Michigan, through Montana,
down Washington state, down the coast. I woke up one morning next to a hippie girl in a VW bus and came into San Francisco on the back of a pickup truck at four in the morning across
the Golden Gate Bridge. That was my first day in California. I'd
never had a day like that. And I just fell in love with this city. I
fell in love with the diversity.

There was a real community, people who struggled. A lot of people were driving a cab and making films—they had all this free time, they could make art when they wanted. I said to myself, *Oh, I want to do that.*

At that time, living at Haight and Divisadero, depending on which direction I walked out of my house, there was a different neighborhood. The Castro was in full bloom, the Western Addition was a black neighborhood, the Upper Haight was the old hippie Haight. My little brother came out one time, and he sat in the window looking out at the intersection for like three hours. He was just like, "I can't believe the kind of people that are just walking around in this street out here."

The other night, I'm sitting in front of the Kabuki Theater in my hybrid taxi, not spewing. I see these two young women coming out of the theater, and I know what they are doing. They pull out their cell phone, and they call either Uber or Lyft, and they are kind of looking at me. I am sitting there, waiting. They kind of chat amongst themselves thinking, *Well, maybe we should . . .* But if you cancel an order with Uber or Lyft, they charge you.

So, sure enough, two or three minutes later, up drives this big Chevy Tahoe, Cadillac Escalade, or whatever it was—some enormous vehicle—and these two girls go scurrying off across the street and hop inside.

If you were to interview those girls, sure as shit they'd be, "Global warming! Let's reduce! Green! We really have to do something! This is our future!" And yet here they are, doing something stupid.

I started to get really interested in clean vehicles after the Kyoto Accords. At that time, I was on the Taxi Commission and thought, *Well, okay. I know I'm in this industry that's burning a lot of gasoline and releasing a lot of carbon. What would it actually mean if I did something in the realm that I was responsible for? What would that actually look like?*

The cab companies were buying old, used police cars and then running them into the ground. Willie Brown, the mayor at the time, the one directive that he ever gave me was, "I want these nasty-ass taxis with the springs coming out of the seat replaced."

So I started to do the calculations: *What would it take to beat Kyoto?* The goal was a 20 percent reduction below 1990 levels by 2012. I sat down, crunched numbers, looked at some of the new vehicles that were out there, the hybrids, did all the carbon numbers. I realized, *If the entire taxi fleet converts to hybrid vehicles, we can pull it off.*

That was the moment. I started to ambulate around Dolores Park, thinking, *How do I write this law?* If I wanted to convert the whole fleet, I had to cover the cost difference between an old used Crown Vic from the SFPD and a new hybrid—about $16,000. So I said, *Okay, drivers are going to be paying, like, $20 or $30 less per night on gas with a hybrid, so we let the companies charge the drivers a surcharge each night. Let's call it $7.50—over the course of three years, that is just about sixteen grand, the cost of the conversion.*

The law passed in 2011, and the mandate kicked in in 2012. We reduced our greenhouse gas emission from about one hundred ten thousand tons to about forty thousand tons in three years by converting the whole fleet to hybrid vehicles. And put four or five thousand in each cabdriver's pockets. So it was a total *win, win, win.*

I was never really recognized for this except for a handful of articles. The city got awards for it, but by this time, the Taxi Commission was disbanded. I got calls like, "Yeah, Paul, we got this award. You really should have been there."

I was at one ceremony inaugurating the clean taxi program.

In the middle of it, the speaker says, "No, no, no. Wait a minute. I see in the audience Paul Gillespie is here. This group of folks, they might be wonderful, but the program came out of the mind of the man sitting in the back row there, Paul Gillespie, former president of the Taxi Commission."

It started a revolution around the country. If you go to Los Angeles, Chicago, New York, they are all trying to do what we did.

A cab is an environmental solution—I've been saying it since I started driving. It allows people to live without a car, without parking. That's why I sold my car. I couldn't find a place to park it in my neighborhood. It was too frustrating.

And the younger generation seems not quite so interested in owning a car—and this is the good part of Uber and Lyft. Young kids don't want a car, they just want mobility. I want the taxi market to capture that, and it's kind of frustrating to see these other companies come in and sort of steal it.

People talk about Uber being so high tech and so progressive, and I'm like, "Man, I have been doing this shit for fifteen years." We were the first to accept credit cards, GPS-based dispatch, workers' comp insurance for drivers. Then, the things I advocate for—clean vehicles, the greenhouse gas reduction mandate—they are all being undermined by Uber and Lyft, which don't do any of those things. They don't have any mandate for clean vehicles, they don't serve wheelchair people or paratransit. Their drivers obviously don't have workers' comp. In fact, it's a nightmare for their drivers. I mean, what if some drunk smashes into you?

I had a woman tell me, "It's just my generation. We're just so used to pulling out our phone and using it for everything. Uber and Lyft just made it so easy." But the taxi apps do the same thing. We just don't store your credit card information and sell it to third parties, telling them where you are going, where you live, where you're going to eat dinner.

The past five years have been hyper in terms of change. And this is ground zero. Now when I go down the street in the Mission here, pretty much everybody looks about the same now. Everybody is young, everybody is white, everybody is in their twenties, everybody is looking at their cell phone. There used to be lesbian bars and weird Indian spice shops and stuff like that. Now, it's like $15 oysters. The clubs are closing, Café du Nord closed, Yoshi's closed. People don't go see live music anymore—that's kind of depressing.

I don't want to go back to the time when there were gangs roaming up and down Nineteenth Street and fifteen different guys selling weed in the park. That was really about all there was in the '90s, but we have to find some kind of balance.

I moved in here, it was $400 a month in '83. Now, I pay $750 and God knows what my guy next door, who just moved in, pays. He is probably paying $2,000 at least for a studio in this neighborhood with a view of the park—maybe more.

He works at a tech company, takes the Google bus on the corner. He sets out his laundry, somebody comes and does his laundry for him. You look down the corner and see the brown people and the poor people waiting for the community bus, and you see this kid waiting for the Google bus. Funny, it is environmentally sound, but it is just the symbolism. That is where we are headed: a whole class of people living a seamless or frictionless life, and they have a series of people working for them.

So my landlord doesn't fix my windows. He doesn't do too much work for me because I am paying $750 a month. But it keeps me in the city. If you are not really focused on making money, there is no place for you in San Francisco—unless you have a rent-controlled apartment or if you have a wealthy boyfriend or girlfriend. Let's face it, my girlfriend is as poor as I am.

I worry about the soul of the city. And I am really conflicted, because everybody wants a dynamic city and a city where bright young people from around the world want to come. We are the envy of other cities in that sense, but are we big enough? Is the city big enough? Is the Bay Area big enough to accommodate all that energy and all that desire and still keep the regular folks, the teachers, the cops, the firemen, the cabdrivers, the restaurant workers? If they have to live in Hercules or Pinole or some of these far-flung places, what happens to the soul of the city?

Nobody wants to have the economy crash, but on the other hand, what are some of these companies? What is Uber really? Why is this company worth $40 billion? People must be thinking they are going to take over the worldwide taxi industry, plus a healthy chunk of UPS and DHL and the local pizza delivery guy, too. And are they really? Now they are trying to align themselves with Google and the driverless cars, saying, *This is going to be our future.*

I love reading, I love making love to my girlfriend, I love traveling. I'm single, and I don't have children or anything like that. I buy books and records and that's about it. I don't have a car. I walk three miles to work every day. I take the Muni. I can afford my lifestyle, which is not real highfalutin.

I still go down every morning and plunk my four quarters in the *Chronicle* box on the corner. If I see a young person reading the newspaper now, on the train, I take a picture. Where is the shared knowledge? What is our common culture? If you are riding the Google bus, and you are looking on your cell phone for stories that are tailored just for you, and at night you are taking an Uber to a nightclub or a restaurant with a lot of other people just like you, where is the interaction with everybody else? Where is the knowledge of what other people are thinking or what's going on in the world?

ELAINE KATZENBERGER

She was working at Bar Vesuvio, before it became "historicized" and the muraled alley outside was renamed as a tribute to Kerouac. She worked there alone in the early mornings, and because there was almost no place else in North Beach open at that hour, she met the neighborhood: poets, old merchant seamen, flamenco dancers, alcoholics on their way to work downtown, taxi drivers having a drink after their shift, and regular folks looking for a good cup of coffee and a little bit of company in those hours before the local cafés opened. And one day a regular offered her a job at a little bookshop across the alley called City Lights. Founded in 1953 by Lawrence Ferlinghetti, a poet in his own right, the store had become a home to literary souls worldwide. Of her first day at work, she says, "It was like stepping into just the right temperature bath water. A stroke of lightning. It's been thirty years."

Today she runs City Lights and oversees its publishing wing, the imprint that first published Allen Ginsberg's *Howl & Other Poems*. In the basement of the bookstore, there are shelves upon shelves of books on progressive politics, labor movements, world history, even a graphic-novel treatment of the Communist Manifesto. Above the main floor, up a set of stairs lined with photographs of poets and writers, is an odd-shaped room labeled POETRY. Her office sits behind an unmarked door.

Back in 2013, when we were all being told that books were going to die out and all the bookstores were going to close, we had our sixtieth anniversary. We'd decided to make the celebration an open house, and the place was just roaring packed. I don't know how many thousands of people came through here that day over the course of four or five hours. We had a few special readings and some party favors on offer, but really it was just about *being here*. It was amazing, very celebratory. Like you feel when you go to a protest and you're surrounded by thousands of people and you think, *Well, thank God. At least for today, right now, I can feel okay.*

When Lawrence founded City Lights, San Francisco wasn't the swinging, bohemian town it would become. That came later. In 1953, San Francisco was a conservative, rather buttoned-up place. And as he tells it, there was a real *need* for a space like City Lights. A place where the poets and writers could congregate and feel welcomed. The bookshop was meant to be a place for people to find *each other*, along with the books.

City Lights is based in a utopian vision of how creativity can be harnessed to make the world a better place, and to make our individual lives better and richer too. It was never thought of as a "business," per se, and in fact, it's always been actively anti-capitalist. The place has always just kept itself going, investing in the people who work here and in the projects we've created and supported over the years. It's about empowerment through knowledge and creativity and about a strong commitment to free inquiry and free expression.

Both the press and the bookstore have always been engaged with the times. So during the 1950s, we published some of the very first books by poets who became the "Beat Generation." During the 1960s and early 1970s, it was resistance to the Vietnam War, the environmental movement, experimenting with spiritual traditions—what's thought of as hippie culture and ideals. In the Reagan years, there were the wars in Central America, anti-nuke movements, and Lawrence was traveling the world, attending poetry festivals and conferences, finding authors and connecting those literary and political dots. It's been more than sixty years now, and inhabiting the line between being a historic institution and being very much a living, breathing participant in contemporary society, that's the dance we do here.

And it seems to resonate. City Lights is full of people, always. And there are people all over the world for whom it's important that City Lights continues to exist. They dream of coming here someday. How many places are like that? It's not like this is Angkor Wat or something. I mean, it's a bookstore. It's uncanny and beautiful, and it's being created each day by the people who work here, and by the people who come to the store and who read the books we publish.

Human beings are looking for collaboration—or commiseration—and *stories*. Even though the experience of writing a book or reading a book can be a very personal and solitary project, a book is a repository of our communal experience. So a bookstore is like a storehouse for our souls.

The story of San Francisco is that it's a boomtown. And boomtowns are never particularly good places to live. Those of us who came here for an alternative to that, we're in the minority now.

San Francisco was always—at least rhetorically, and sometimes in action—a kind of community unto itself. Maybe it still is. But if San Francisco no longer represents an idea of humanism and freedom from the treadmill, then where do we fit in? What's our role?

The thing is, we are still *here*. And by working to keep this place strong amid everything else that's going on—we're reminding people that there is still another way to be.

I've had a recurring nightmare—where I'll come walking down the street and it's like Tokyo or Times Square. All the buildings are tall, there's neon and huge video advertising everywhere. And it's a terrible feeling: *Oh my God, what has happened?*

And then, finally, there's City Lights. It's still there. Just this little sweet building surrounded by all of it. And once I see it, I can breathe again.

CAROL QUEEN

She moved to San Francisco after college and soon enrolled in the Institute for Advanced Study of Human Sexuality. "There was a room with a screen in the front—a television the size of a Volkswagen—and a bunch of pillows, on the ground—the '70s were into this—and all day long the representatives of varying sexualities ranged before me to explore, like a set of Star Wars figurines. It felt like San Francisco was convened to make a sexually diverse space." She self-describes as a "cultural sexologist," and writes, speaks, and organizes around sex-positivity as a political and social movement. She taught sex education in the 1980s, bringing her face-to-face with the AIDS epidemic. She witnessed firsthand how the queer community was both shattered and rebuilt through crisis, a story common to many communities in San Francisco.

t's important to know more about each other. It's important to be close to people who aren't like you, to develop understandings about likeness and unlikeness that help you see why we go in different directions. Even if you never get to what makes us the way we are—*are we born that way,* all that stuff, even if you never go all that far—there's still value to thinking about the way we are brought together or pulled apart.

When the AIDS crisis began, there had essentially been two separate communities—with not many points of intersection.

Many, many gay men or queer men or bi men knew hardly any lesbians; plenty of lesbians I knew wouldn't talk to guys at all, gay or not. That has almost entirely changed. And it was HIV that changed it.

The discourse initially within the women's community was, "This is not our problem, except insofar as we can see all this homophobic writing on the wall will probably wash up at our feet." And: "If those guys hadn't gone to the baths and been all wild and crazy, this wouldn't be happening to them either." That was the stigma. And of course, attached was, "And now you bisexuals are going to give it to us." So I picked an awesome time to come out as bi.

But I started to understand that I could function as a bridge character. I could take that knowledge and go into straight communities, talk about their exposure and at the same time do the work of unpacking their fears about AIDS victims, their homophobia . . .

There was something about this moment, something like: *we are all in the soup because of sex*. Here's our little town on the edge of the cliff, in an earthquake zone, and HIV jacked up that feeling. You can't have the kind of an impact that AIDS had on a city the size of San Francisco and not have it felt everywhere, *everywhere*.

There was a fundamental shift in how anybody who wasn't living a heteronormative life understood their community space. There began to be trans people coming out and coming together, the kinky people versus the not-kinky people. Women that didn't care that there were gay men in the same city found that they cared if the men were dropping like flies. Because HIV asked all non-heteronormative people to say, "We are in this together. There's something meaningful for us collectively to get out of the work."

It was a national happening—on the heels of this great politicization around sex and difference and identities, this crisis turned everybody into some kind of stakeholder. Even if they were just a homophobic, AIDS-phobic asshole, the more upset they were, the more of a stakeholder they were. San Francisco's identity just gave everyone an excuse to talk about it more. Solidarity in the community was forged in crisis.

Had I not lived through this, and lived through it *in this city*—I would have wound up in some variant life, an alternate universe to this, but I would not have ended up in this one. I would not have written what I've written. I would not have spoken the way I've spoken. I would not have made the relational choices I've made. I could not have been the *me* that I am right now if I had not come to San Francisco during that time.

Today, people from other parts of the country—parts that have never been part of our story—are moving here and bringing their own communities' cultures in, and we have to blend somehow. They are from more culturally conservative places, which is changing the understanding of what it means to live here. It's getting more expensive. Even the wealthy people in the queer and sex community now are not the most radical politically. Which I think is conservatizing the whole city.

It is a new wave. It happened to the communities who lived here when we arrived. But this feels like the first generation that has not come here for *San Francisco* specifically. I'm sure a lot of them are excited to be here: *I hope I get a job. Look at all the tech there is!* But they aren't here to discover what came before them. They would have gone to any city where the job opportunities and career culture offered the same prospects.

I walk around Hayes Valley with the straight kids and the real expensive baby strollers, and I think to myself, *They think it's getting better. They think it's getting better.* And of course their older brothers and sisters are still living in their parents' basement because they can't pay off their student loans. So,

sure, from that perspective it is. But they are kind of libertarian dicks.

I am here to remind people that there are other perspectives.
You can't tell me that a whole bunch of young people have just
moved into San Francisco and they're not interested in exploring
sexuality, because that hasn't happened in many, many, many
decades—if ever. And I feel it is my job to keep the doors open,
remind them that this city has a political legacy, and a rich, multifaceted sex history, and encourage them to *yes, come play!*

Today, queers are running to get married, and heterosexuals
are trying to learn how to do polyamory properly. I mean, *what
does that tell you?* People who never had a question whether or
not they were going to live a straight life are trying pretty hard
to make a place where they don't have to live one.

DO D.A.T.

He was a founding member of the Attik, an Oakland hip-hop group.
"Eclectic . . . eclectic treasures. We were trying to elevate the consciousness higher. The Bay Area was the attic of California, and
L.A. was the basement." When the group broke up, he stepped out
as a solo artist and educator in the community. His latest album is
titled *Oakland in Blue*.

East Oakland is kinda hot. It's clicking in a different kinda way. The
energy—you're gonna wanna have your head on a swivel a
little bit more and just kinda pay attention to what's goin' on
around you. It's polar: you've got the Panthers and the pimps,

you have the protesters and the profiteers. The two pillars of the community, and everything kinda spreads out from there.

I didn't grow up *in* the shit, but I grew up, like, *up the street* from the shit. So it wouldn't take much for me to get down there and get into it. I could see, *Oh, okay . . . Bro is selling drugs. Homeboy just got shot.*

My parents told me that East Oakland looked a lot like San Leandro when they first moved up here: it was a nice area. Then all that shit went down. Their oldest kids were part of the generation that got hit hard by crack. My brother was familiar with that element, but thank God, he and my sister didn't get caught up in it. But all of their friends, all the folks that graduated school in 1980, 1981, they almost got wiped out. Wiped *out*.

Paying attention, being young, I saw where we was living. There were seven or eight corner stores between Seventy-Third and Eighty-Second. Oakland ain't that big. That's a very concentrated area to have all that. Those stores represent . . . oppression. They represent *convenience*, which is a different type of oppression if you think about it. It can *turn into* oppression.

I feel like America is good at creating sociopaths. Greed is running this country. Greed *and* Fear. It's like these two entities take turns, they're a tag team. Maybe Fear is really the big boss, but Greed is the main manufacturer of individuals who can't or won't take in their environment, or realize how much space they're taking up.

The city is changing. Uptown district, there wasn't shit up there but one club in 2002, 2003—wasn't nothing else going on. But they were very community-oriented.

You get a couple more bars. Jerry Brown puts in that school. All of a sudden it's not so friendly to hip-hop. They don't want us there. Whatever silly associations they have with hip-hop culture, or rappers, or whatever.

Second and MacArthur, that's gonna look a lot different now, the soon-to-be Uber building and all that represents.* It's just a sign of the times. A tombstone. *Take, take, take.* These are individuals that had an idea, and they hustled it, but there's also that endless consumption, endless hunger. A very American kind of thing. *Gotta get it for me!* Ironic, but also very American.

What did Richard Wright say? Being *of* America but not being *American*. Like, being able to be in America but not being able to really participate. The same narrative retold, over and over again. This time it's with the tech industry.

Oakland was a major jazz and blues hub. Anybody that was doing music came through to the Bay Area. They would do a big show in San Francisco, but they would come to Oakland to kick it.

Right across the street from the Seventh Street Post Office was Esther's Orbit Room. It was known around the world. B. B. King, Bobby "Blue" Bland, Miles Davis, all these other folks, they would come to this little hole-in-the-wall joint, and they would perform. I grew up around spots like that.

Oakland in Blue is encompassing that tradition—different producers, my peers, the best I knew, working on each track—different sounds, something jazzy, then a hood-open feel, then go to something like Bourbon Street, then a straight-up hip-hop sound. It was a metaphor, different artists reflecting different facets of Oakland.

It's kinda cool driving through. If you take MacArthur from 106th all the way down to the lake, and you go down International, it's interesting watching the city change. So you're in

---

* Uber abandoned its Oakland headquarters in 2017.

Fruitvale, and that's where a lot of Latinos are. Between Fairfax, that's where all the black people are. Then you get closer down to the lake and that's more where the Asian and Pacific Islanders are.

So the album was taking a specific color, green, and expanding it out to all the different kinds of green you can get. Or *Blue*. And painting with that. We much more than hyphy and Too Short. We Hieroglyphics. We Goapele. We Tony! Toni! Toné! We Sly and the Family Stone. We Duke and B. B. and Miles.

Oakland is the heartbeat. It resonates outward into the rest of the Bay Area. San Francisco is a city built to funnel all the resources from the area. But there wouldn't be a San Francisco without an Oakland to take from. I mean . . . slaves built the White House.

EDWIN LINDO

He sits in a playground atop a hill in Bernal Heights, near his grandmother's home where he grew up. He slept next to the washer-dryer in the basement. Years later, the house passed to a family member, who quickly filed for eviction against Edwin and his father. "There are people who say that this is a family issue. But this is the epitome of what we're dealing with today. Because if it wasn't for what that house is now worth—$1.4 million—they wouldn't be evicting us. It just shows that it doesn't even matter if you're family, this is how ugly it is getting." A twelve-year saga unfolded, hauling father and son into housing court over and over again, inspiring him to go to law school and turning him into an eviction expert. When the case settled, he chose to stay in the same neighborhood, just blocks from his family home. Sitting in the swings, he looks out over most of the Mission, Noe Valley, and up toward Potrero Hill.

I can see everything in my story from up on this hill.

My grandparents came here in 1962, before the civil war in Nicaragua. They were janitors at Wonder Bread, when Wonder Bread was still in this neighborhood, in this city. My grandfather retired from there, and my grandmother worked for maybe ten years more. But they saved up some money, bought a home for $17,000, in Bernal Heights.

My dad's first job was shoe-shining on Mission Street, and he was so proud of it. Then he had a paper route and said he was the fastest paper-route deliverer: "I got a raise." As a kid, he played with Carlos Santana and Carlos Santana's brother in Dolores Park across the street from Mission High School. Hearing them jam out when they started their bands, *malo* coming out of their window.

My mom and dad met right down the street, there. They were dancing. He was much older than her, but that's my dad.

I went to school over by Third Street. I would wake up, run down the block, catch the 24 down to the 9 to San Bruno, jumping on the back and not paying because I didn't have enough money. We would go to those basketball courts and play pickup, or watch the big guys play sports at St. Mary's or Portola, hoping one day we could be as good as them, never once thinking of going to college, because that wasn't on my radar. After that going to the corner store, buying Cheeto chips with food stamps that I pulled out of a coupon book and feeling awkward because they had to change the register for me—someone grouching that I was holding up the line. Running through all these streets, talking nonsense, hearing every language but English, getting home in the freezing cold with the fog rolling in.

I realize for many people, this is all they are, memories. Inherently there is no value to them. There's no tangible currency that you can attach to them. It doesn't make anyone money. It doesn't buy you a house. It doesn't do anything unless you open up and appreciate that there's much more to value than the currency in your bank account.

In just the last three months, there have been 220 evictions in the city, 50 in the Mission. Over the past, I think, five years, there's been a 220 percent increase in the eviction rate.

Many of these are "no fault" evictions: an opportunity for a landlord, under law, to exit the rental market, for no reason whatsoever except that they no longer want to be landlords. Which means they have the opportunity to convert into condos and sell them—because now you're no longer a *landlord,* you're an *owner.*

What does that mean for the people who are tenants in these neighborhoods? It means that though they pay rent on time—they've never violated the lease, they've done nothing wrong—they get a notice saying their tenancy is now terminated. They have to leave.

Statutorily they're given an amount, a relocation amount—that, I think, today, is a $15,000 maximum per *unit,* not per *person.* But many of these homes have more than three people living in them. So you have less than $5,000 per person to survive an eviction. That doesn't cover attorney costs.

Are there places where these people can even afford to live? Once they're evicted, there's nowhere to go. San Francisco is an inelastic market. We are surrounded by water. There's nowhere to build but down or up.

We have to be deliberate—and transparent—about what population we are trying to serve. The mayor is saying we need to build 5,000 new units every year. This is right after the Budget Analyst's Office of San Francisco said that to even have an effect on rental prices, we have to build *100,000* new units. So is market-rate housing going to solve the affordability crisis—or do we need to focus on building not *more* housing but *affordable* housing?

We need to serve the population that has been evicted, the population that can't afford to live here, or they're gonna be spending their *entire income* on housing.

I am drafting legislation for a moratorium in the Mission. It's not an indefinite moratorium. Legally it can only be eighteen months, and it has to further the cause of preventing any harm to the public, to safety, to the welfare of the city. Many of those criteria can be met. Studies have to be done to understand the populations that are being affected and what they need.

Because there is a dual social experience happening now. You have people who come here and work in tech, who live in a condo, maybe been here for about a year, and never meet someone who grew up here. The flip side of that is you have people who work in the local taqueria, or they work as a bus driver. They're born and raised here, have three kids here, and they've never met a tech worker. I don't want to isolate those two groups, but that tends to be the conversation nowadays.

Someone says, "You know what? I make a difference. I have five employees. I pay them. I pay my taxes. I pay business taxes. And I contribute every time I go out to eat dinner, every time I use my dry cleaner."

That's great. How long have you been here? You've been here two years, great. Now, there's a woman that has lived here for thirty-five years. She has three jobs, working minimum wage. She's a single mother of three kids. All those three kids go into public school. Now, the taxes that she's been paying for thirty-five years, let's add those up. Let's add the money from the federal government the public school gets every time her kids sit in a chair. Let's add up the fact that they buy locally, within, I'd say, a four- or five-block radius from where they live. Every dollar they spend goes right back into the community, whether buying produce at the market, paying the salary for an employee who's probably someone who lives right next to her. So if we weigh that out, I'm gonna say that she has you beat.

People like her hold this city up, because if we wiped the slate clean of all middle- and low-income families, we won't have an economic floor to stand on. You push them out—tech bust happens—all you have left is U-Penn graduates with a degree in sociology who can only find a job waiting tables. And they're not going to accept $15 an hour.

So this actually hurts everyone—from the folks who are getting displaced to the ones who are living in the tallest building in the downtown skyline and don't have enough time to cook their own food.

San Francisco wants San Franciscans that say, "I want to be here forever." Not that we don't want new faces, but we can't start displacing permanent residents for temporary ones. Because when they leave, we'll be left with a gaping hole.

It's easy to turn a blind eye and say, "But look at San Francisco. It's so beautiful." But you judge a city not by how it treats those that are doing well. Let's go into the hood, let's go to Bayview, Hunters Point, let's go to the Alemany Projects, let's go to Double Rock. Why is it that we have twenty thousand homeless students attending schools in the San Francisco Unified School District? There's an underworld that we've built, and that we continue to live in.

So let's walk down a path to a viable city. And that vision is only possible when the city cares for the people who maintain its foundations.

That's where the public sector comes in. The public sector has to be just as innovative as the tech sector, perhaps even more so. A lot of these things are inextricably bound. They need to help us create a shared vision of how we can all live together.

MARGARET ZHAO

She grew up in the Richmond, a residential neighborhood in the northeast of San Francisco, running along Golden Gate Park to the Pacific. She went to school on the East Coast, thinking she might stay there. But she returned and made her career in tech. She now lives in an old townhouse blocks from her childhood home. She is curled up on the sofa covered in blankets.

The Richmond was one of the last bastions against true gentrification. I wouldn't say it's really working class. But it's normal people. It's not affluent. Not a lot of people move to San Francisco to live in the Richmond. You had a lot of families, a lot of single-family homes that people owned outright because they'd lived there a long, long time. Only recently, when I tell people that I was born here, they're like, "Oh, wow. That's so rare."

When I was growing up here, it was mostly Asian families, I think. In the early '90s, post–Soviet Union, a lot of Russians moved in. The first Russian bakery opened up, and I remember in elementary school tasting this heavy rye bread for the first time.

None of my friends were in the Richmond growing up because I went to a private school in Pac Heights. A fancy girls' school for old, WASPy San Francisco. I carpooled with the one other girl who also lived in the Richmond.

For me, it was never a thing. I never thought of us as being not wealthy and other people wealthy. I was so used to us being different from everybody else in every respect that it didn't particularly bother me. It was sort of like, *Oh, they choose to have big houses. We choose to have a little house because it's cozy.*

Both of my parents found themselves here after having led very itinerant lives. They both had sort of refugee-type experiences, and so they really didn't want me to have the same, to have to switch schools all the time, to have to move. So they stayed put.

It's weird now to be moving back to the Richmond. It's very bizarre—I feel conflicted—being part of this first wave of change. I'm gentrifying my own neighborhood. How weird is that? I am moving back to the place where I grew up in very different circumstances. I'm not going to live the same way. I have different ideas about what I want from a neighborhood, I spend my time differently. Isn't that kind of a mind fuck?

Growing up, there was no "scene" at all, it wasn't a young person's city. "Bohemian" meant my friend's parents, who were schoolteachers and had a house covered in artifacts from their travels. I remember seeing the first hipster clothing stores on the main drag in the Richmond and just being like, "I can't believe they can sustain that now." When I was growing up, it was really just food stores. It was Chinese markets and dollar stores and stuff. Now there are wine bars.

There was this very sad event recently—this old Lebanese grocery store closed. It took me years to go inside, probably twenty years. The windows are filled with stuff, you don't think that there's going to be anything appealing inside, but then you go in and there's amazing homemade halva and baklava, big blocks of it, it's just delicious. Now it's some brewpub.

No one is going to open a Middle Eastern grocery store there anymore. There isn't a place for that. People's tastes are getting more and more similar—neighborhoods are looking more and more alike—no one could run a store where you don't open up your windows so people can see what's inside, where it feels like you're a hoarder.

The city is so inarticulate about identity, so overly polite about conflict, and yet is dealing with an amorphous cloud of change right now. Everybody sort of looks the same. They kind of dress the same. We don't know who is a billionaire, but we know some of them are. And if you're *from* here, *your* world is changing, *you* can't move, but *they* can. I imagine that feeling is exceptionally terrifying.

IDEXA

She runs Black and Blue Tattoo, right on the border between the Mission and the Castro. She's known for her abstract work: "I'm trying to find it on their body. I'm not really creating something; I believe it's already there, and I'm just bringing it out. I think Michelangelo said this, the form is already in the stone, and you're just finding it." She came from Germany to California as a teenager, hitchhiking all the way from Los Angeles to San Francisco. We sit behind the shop, drinking herbal tea in a garden.

grew up in a very homogenous society that I never quite felt like I was part of or fit into. I think a lot of people feel like that about their communities.

When I was twenty-five, I moved here for good and changed my name. My given name is Stefanie, and I was Steffi growing up in Germany. And then once I became an adult, I didn't fit it anymore. When I moved here, people started calling me Stef, and it was almost right. Idexa is derived from the German word for lizard. Some people call me Dex, which feels even better.

People kind of made space for me. I'd never experienced that. I always felt like I worked really hard to create a little bit of space for myself, a little niche that I could breathe in. I came here and came out really heavy-duty into S&M, and I started tattooing pretty much right away, people kind of went, *Ooh, here you are. I'll move over a little bit.* I just kind of stepped up and into that space. And opened my shop when I was twenty-nine.

People often ask, "How did you think of opening a woman's shop?" It's like, well, if you're a feminist and you're a dyke and you surround yourself with women, it's not far-fetched at all. We opened right next to Red Dora's Bearded Lady, a lesbian café.

Also I came from a culture where women were allowed to separate in a way. We had women's bookshops in Germany, we had women's stores. Men weren't allowed, and it was legal. The mailman got yelled at for coming inside.

We got a lot of resistance. It always felt like there was a tattoo mafia. I didn't know if it was the Hells Angels, the old guard. They were assholes and they could be assholes.

It was exciting to have a place where men didn't assume that it was their place. And we had the clientele that didn't feel comfortable going to the other shops. Tons of people who were like, "I got tattooed there and felt horrible." Many men wanted to be tattooed by us. Young fags, even grown straight men, where they just felt like, "Those are not my people and I don't feel taken care of." It opened my eyes to how many men felt uncomfortable with that kind of machismo.

I really felt every tattoo artist should be into S&M. Because they should know about consensuality, about taking somebody through an intensive experience, about negotiating, about rites of passage. I had a dream of a tattoo shop that was a lot more spiritual.

It's funny, the Mission used to be "our space." It was lesbians in the Mission and the fags in the Castro. But before that, the Mission belonged to Latinos. I didn't speak Spanish. I wasn't part of that culture in a way where I could feel good about taking apartments away from them.

Now my rent is a lot higher than it used to be. When I moved into this new space, my rent was probably a third of what I'm paying now. And it's only been twelve years. There's no limit in commercial stuff. Landlords can just raise it to $20,000, and people just have to move. There's no protection.

So it's always happening. It's just a little too easy to distance yourself from it and not take any responsibility. I'm definitely part of it and I'm even profiting from it. Now if you don't have a tattoo, you're an outsider. And we're a high-end shop. It's great that people have money, and it's great that people have credit cards. We're not a used bookstore that has to leave. We're still here.

We're holding on. We're from a shipwreck, and I actually have a piece of wood.

Oh, it's horrible what's happening. People get kicked out. You hear buildings are being set on fire so they can get rid of people. You see people digging in the trash cans. But it's also beautiful. There's been a lot of money put into the neighborhood and into the buildings. Buildings that would have fallen apart have been renovated.

Oh, it's the end of the world soon. We're not the first generation who thinks that. There's always a reason. There's always the doom. There's always the movement that kicks out the weak.

That doesn't mean it's okay, but it's not *new*. It's important to be conscious of the cycle that's been going on forever. There's no bad guy or good guy. We all participate in it. It's really hard to make changes on a bigger level.

I'm a lot less militant than I used to be. I really disappeared from the streets when I started tattooing. I don't want to go to protests anymore. I can't afford being locked up. I have kids, I have a business. I'm not too sad about it because when I lived like that I was very anxious. It was exhausting.

I'm a little bit more of a homebody these days. I love simplicity now. And I am with a man, which is not boring to me anymore. We have a great relationship, a family. It's very colorful and very multifaceted. I don't need to play or have sex with somebody else in order to be fulfilled, which is fairly new for me. I don't need to be challenged every minute of the day to prove that I'm capable. I don't have to prove anything anymore, which is really nice. I've been really lucky.

And the S&M community seems a lot straighter than it used to. I've always felt in the middle of the gender spectrum, and even straight people kind of get that these days. Which I find exciting. But of course, it also washes out the essence, when stuff gets mainstreamed. It makes it less threatening for people, it becomes something more normal.

BILL FISHER

In the 1930s, his family opened a pawnshop downtown. Over the years, the shop grew. They counted famous artists, boxers, and actors among their clients. Eventually he took over the shop. There are three glass cases full of jewelry, watches, and rare coins. Musical instruments hang silent on pegs. He sits in the back, desk covered in paper, family photos on the wall, and a six-foot iron safe behind him.

W*e're here for people that don't have money or don't have ID—or* don't have enough ID that they can open a bank account. That's our function.

People have the Rod Steiger look in their mind, think I'm that guy from *The Pawnbroker*. Even my friends say things like, "Can you bring a diamond home?" So you have that stigma. But I am very private. My father taught me years and years ago: *Stay low.* You'll do a better job, and you'll look better. *Don't make enemies, because you might meet them on the way down.* We've been very, very lucky.

With the economy, I've started to feel bad. The fall can happen quickly. I see my customers' names in the newspaper at this party or that party. Some have loads and loads of money on paper, but no cash. They can't go to the bank. Or real-estate brokers, they have to spend the money to look the part. People drive up in their Mercedes and pawn their Rolex wristwatch. They don't have the money to keep up with the game.

I've started really hating my business—crying. Families are getting kicked out by landlords. My Spanish customers, Hispanic customers, three generations or more—are going somewhere else. I talk to them about their family. I *know* their family. "My daughter, she just got married." Or they'll call me up, "I just want to let you know that my husband passed away."

I'm like a doctor. We do a lot of good for a lot of people. I'm not going to fold my business up. We're going to stay.

LYMAN HOLLINS

A former longshoreman who was born and raised in the area, he points to all the signs of change: the black church fielding noise complaints from recent transplants, the new development down-town that is all shopping but no affordable housing, no schools. He calls it "Manifest Destiny made local." And thinks nowhere is it more apparent than along the San Francisco waterfront, where the shipping industry once thrived and he worked as a longshoreman.

was texting a friend, trying to say "gentrifying neighborhood." And my spell check corrected it to "terrifying neighborhood." And it took me a couple times to get it right, because it kept on replacing "gentrifying" with "terrifying."

I used to love going down to the port. As a kid, we'd go down to the union hall in San Francisco, near Pier 39, and hang out there with my dad. And the guys would be playing cards and dominoes waiting for a job to come. A lot of these guys—that was their life, that or the bar. *Work, work, work.*

Friday mornings, we'd go out to the city early, seven o'clock in the morning. The longshoremen had their pay window at the Ferry Building. My dad would pick up his paycheck. Then we'd head further south, down Third—and there was the life of the port, industrial life, happening. The warehouses and the rail tracks. Trains and trucks and motion and movement.

But then, the waterfront started closing up. The city started losing worksites. Workers were retiring. The union wasn't hiring anyone new. Modernization and mechanization. And nothing has really resolved, right? Everything's still in motion . . . which is too bad. Because that's the place that I grew up.

Now it's brick and steel and cement. Office buildings, tech buildings, apartment buildings, bars, restaurants. It's just . . .

eerie. I'm thinking, *This is a neighborhood . . . this is a neighborhood now with people doing things.* But there's not the same motion that was happening before. It feels like a tomb.

My dad signed up as a longshoreman in the late '60s, early '70s. There was so much work in San Francisco. They needed people to unload cargo. And if you were willing to keep on showing up, you worked your way up. So he stuck it out. There were lean times, times when there wasn't much work; you had to tighten your belt and trust that it was gonna get better. But you thought, *It had been better before, so it was gonna get better again.*

He was sensitive, gregarious, social, adaptable—open to speaking to different kinds of people, and able to be in different environments. But it was still odd to see him in this whole other environment with a bunch of hard-drinking, gambling long-shoremen. There was a respect for him. People would, you know, smile when they saw him. The same kind of feeling that I had for him. And at the union hall, I realized he had these options. I thought, *He could be sitting here all night long, but he comes home.*

He worked nights and would take us to school in the morning, pick us up from school in the afternoon. If there was some issue at school, he would be the one that would be available. People talk about the sacrifices that men make when they stay home, having to give up this or give up that. My dad just did it—like it was very natural. Whether or not he enjoyed it, whether or not he was exhausted, whether or not he hated it and cursed us every day, we never felt it. It was just what he did.

When my father got sick and passed away, his book passed to me. A union book is both literal and metaphorical—it states that you're a member and has your plug number, but it's almost a simplified passport to a whole way of life. I had the opportunity to go in as a longshoreman.

And I was kind of like, *Oh, well, this is great. I could do this for a couple years, you know? Sock some money away, and then figure out where to go from there.* Twelve years later, I was still doing it. Still a longshoreman. Bought a house. Traveled a lot. Lived quite happily, I think.

I met a whole bunch of old men who were contemporaries of my father. A lot of older black men, who were kind of extensions of him. A lot of them had grown up in the South, or their family had moved here from the South. They had come to California because they heard there were jobs, or they heard about free schools for their kids, free college, or they heard you could build a life as a black man. So they had very similar stories to my father's. Suddenly, I was sitting with those men as their contemporary, all working alongside each other.

It was a weird experience: to walk in the same places, to wear his overalls, to do some of the same jobs, work with the same people. It was very comforting.

A ship came in late one day, at a new terminal that I hadn't worked yet. We're sitting in the parking lot waiting for the ship to get tied in, it was a foggy day. And somebody comes out and starts just yelling, "I need to see Lyman! Is Lyman around here? I heard Lyman's here. . . ."

And I'm like, "I'm Lyman." I'm wearing my dad's old overalls—they say *Lyman.* I'm a junior.

And he's like, "I knew your dad. Come with me."

"For what?"

"Shut up. I'm gonna show you how to drive something."

On the waterfront, if you drive heavy equipment, you get paid more—and you catch better breaks. And so, because of this guy's respect for my father, he gave me this opportunity.

There was a huge variety of people on the waterfront. There were people who had law degrees who still were putting in a few hours a month as a longshoreman to maintain benefits and things. People who were architects, retired train engineers.

More women started coming down, coming from other jobs and bringing those experiences.

There's nothing like three o'clock in the morning on a container ship, breaking loose a few bays of cargo, removing all these heavy iron rods. Sweaty, greasy, hanging out with a bunch of men of different ages, black men, talking about life. Not competing for money, not competing for a different position, just bullshitting. Politics, love, life, school, friends, your family, the white man. All of those things, but in this amazing, sometimes bizarre, setting.

Especially when you're out on the terminals closest to the end of Seventh Street, and you have this amazing view of San Francisco and the Bay Bridge and the lights. You're sitting up high. Thinking, *Wow, it just doesn't get better than this. They're paying me for this. To be here with these people in this moment. Yes, it's true: it's three o'clock in the morning. I'm freezing. I'm wet from sweat. But I am not stuck in an office someplace. I am not programming right now. I'm in communion and in community with people.*

PART III

THE BALKANIZATION OF THE BAY

S ome ask why the public sector hasn't offered better solutions, or why local government hasn't intervened with more energy. Others place the burden on those new to the city to take a stronger role in the community, integrate better, volunteer more—or on the leaders of the tech industry to clean up the mess in their own wake. Some even dare to point the finger at the old city and the displaced or at the activists and organizers—*if only there was a greater outcry, if only we heard from them more, if only they made more noise, something could be done.* Many blame "the technology" itself: *if we want "progress," we have to resign ourselves to the trouble it brings.* To them, we have seen this movie here before, and we will see it again.

The deeper the change cuts, the more it destroys the weapons available to combat it. City Hall has to search for new sources of funding as old wells dry up. At home, breadwinners look for new jobs, adapt to new ways of working, as technology and the gig economy make most careers less stable. Competition in the tech industry keeps leaders, even middle managers, preoccupied with their own struggle and either unable or unwilling to stoop and dig through the problems at their feet. Many of our fundamental assumptions about what makes a city work, what knits a community together, are being challenged—even the ability for neighbors, friends, and family to provide for one another in times of need. It is as if everyone has focused for so long on their own problems that they've grown civically nearsighted and lost the ability to see across the city, across the street, even next door.

RICHARD WALKER

An "economic geographer" with radical tendencies, he was naturally drawn to UC Berkeley. He devoted his career to studying the evolution of the Bay Area, how its economy and environment shaped each other hand in hand.

One of the great puzzles of the world is what's called the "Resource Curse." Why so many places with abundant resources—like the Congo, like Jamaica, like West Virginia—end up poor. The Bay Area is founded on the same mythology—the '49ers, the Gold Rush, the idea that the Golden Gate is the outpost of Western civilization . . . These are stories trumpeted by the sons and daughters of the Bohemian Club—but to a surprising degree the myths are true.*

---

* A private club that meets in secret and whose members include global leaders in business, politics, and the arts.

So how did California escape the curse? What were the social and political conditions that led to this incredible prosperity?

One is that capital stuck to a lot of hands. Wealth stayed in California and got reinvested in a capitalist manner. First in agriculture. Then in manufacturing, mining. Then in agricultural equipment and the canning industry. These industries built San Francisco and the Bay Area.

Another is skilled labor in abundance. It wasn't just the rich elite who built this incredibly fecund, dynamic economy, and it wasn't the miners—a lot of them died with nothing. The new capitalists were educated. Skilled machinists. People who were innovative. People who could get a lot of money in their hands, could be given a long leash, and could revolutionize an industry. The Caterpillar tractor was invented in the Bay Area, the bulldozer was invented in the Bay Area. These are amazing things that nobody remembers anymore. It's not just the silicon chip.

The third pillar is the mass influx of good labor, good workers, people to man the factories, the fields, the mines. It cost more to get to California, so we tended to get a different cut. These were white and European workers, then the Chinese, then Mexicans and Filipinos and Japanese—everyone under the sun. And unlike South Texas or the Cotton South, the critical difference in California was the racial turnover. We never developed a permanent racial underclass. Don't get me wrong, there are lots of racisms in the world, and California's is no less serious. But the exploitation in California cut across race.

So we had the best of all possible worlds. Massive amounts of money—makes life easier—that's reinvested in the region. Skilled labor to use the money to innovate. And mass immigration, wave after wave of educated people who could do the shit work. The three pillars that built California.

And it gave us the independence to build the culture and politics that allowed us to protect what we had built. We were an outlier city, we had money, we had autonomy, and we were a port, so we had intercourse with the world. So this was always a place that had a very "uppity" working class and "uppity" populace who would revolt against the seizure of power by the capitalists and by the elite: and they have done that several times, whether it was the Union Labor Party or the Workingmen's Party or the Progressives or the unions of the '30s, and so on.

There was also always a very strong countercultural movement, and I include in that a culture of sin. They weren't just a bunch of poets, but were connected with the working class, going against the mainstream bluenoses, bourgeois propriety, and so on. San Francisco always had that—that thread runs all the way through. It helped attract people like Ferlinghetti and the Beats, conscientious objectors, gays in the '70s, and so on. Even earlier, the first real movement for suffrage was in California, sometime in the 1890s.

Electronic technology is just another goldmine. In a sense, unleashing and controlling the power of the electron is no different than digging in the ground, smelting, *yada, yada, yada.* The nineteenth century looks primitive today, and we'll look primitive in a hundred years. The Elon Musk effect, the Travis Kalanick obsession—they're just the lucky sons of guns who staked their claim on the right river. And it's produced a volcanic eruption of money.

There's reinvestment: a lot of money gets plowed back into tech. Hell, since the housing meltdown in 2008, the global economy is so shitty, a lot of the world's surplus money gets buried in tech because it doesn't know what else to do. There's plenty of skilled labor. From all over the world, smart people from Hong Kong, Australia, France, you name it, they're in Silicon Valley coming up with new ideas, new products, and feeding the engine.

The problem is the working class. A few hundred thousand

professionals may think they make the Bay Area great, but they forget about all the people doing the other work: taking care of our kids, teaching in our schools, running government offices, being secretaries, health-care professionals, right up to doctors in local hospitals. We have a giant working class—a working class of color. The bottom 80 percent of the population, 3 million active workers plus their families. And those people still count.

A third of the workers in the Bay Area aren't paid a living wage. Rent and food and the essentials are extremely expensive now and aren't getting any cheaper. The average wage in the Bay Area is quite high—but that's inflated by the filthiness of the super-rich. The average worker does better in Atlanta, or Houston. Plus, California was the center of the housing bubble, and when it burst a lot of people were caught in the fallout. It's a mess. Now, the higher prices rise, the more they are squeezed. They are pushed to the periphery, two-, three-hour commutes. Or worse, driven out of the Bay Area.

The whole region is skating on very thin ice, despite its immense wealth. We are multiplying millionaires, billionaires, sure. But it is hard to regenerate your workforce under these conditions. If the working class can't live within reach of their jobs. If young people cannot afford to put down roots. We are destroying the basis of our prosperity. We are eating our children.

ALEX KAUFFMANN

He runs an experimental design team at Google, where he helped build Google Glass and invent Cardboard, Google's low-fi virtual reality player. In his spare time, he tinkers around, learning how to cook exotic foods from scratch and experimenting with human-to-dolphin communication. We drink free coffee from the Google cafeteria.

just wanted to learn how to do something with my hands. And a friend said, you should check out this program at NYU. So I went home and looked up "ITP," the Interactive Telecommunications Program. It was like somebody had gone into my dreams and constructed the perfect graduate program. I didn't know something like that existed. And once I did, I couldn't think of anything else.

I literally applied the same night. It's the only time in my life that I've been able to write a two-thousand-word essay in, like, twenty-five minutes. I knew exactly what I wanted to do: I wanted to build something that acts on the world. I was tired of doing passive stuff, I wanted to make something that catalyzes.

My goals going into ITP were two. One was to learn enough circuit design that I can get a lightbulb to turn on and off at will. And to learn enough programming that I can make something move around a screen.

So my first day of school, I had Introduction to Physical Computing, which is hardware design, and Introduction to Computational Media, which is programming. And in hardware design we learned how to light up a lightbulb, and in computational media we learned how to move a thing around a screen. So: done. The next two years were pure icing.

I remember various platitudes in undergrad where people would say, "You're learning how to learn." At ITP you were learning how to *do.* "Oh, here's how you put together a nuclear turbine." And guess what: even rocket science is not rocket science. You read the book, and if you don't get it, doesn't matter. Start playing.

I was recruited in New York. And sure, San Francisco was familiar because I'd been here before. My mom always used to say—and I think this is sort of a '60s, '70s view of California—you pick up the US and you shake it, and whatever isn't nailed down ends up in San Francisco. I think that's what happened: all the rolling stones landed and gathered moss here. Because the weather is perfect and because there was lots of land and it was cheap and it was groovy.

Now you have this influx of a very brittle, very rational, and extremely practical population taking over. And the two of them, they don't know how to talk to each other. San Francisco is a city of two extremes. And the normal people get drowned out, don't they? I mean, *I* don't know any of them.

Americans—in general, but especially in big cities—they express themselves through spending. Like a worm expresses the dirt through its body—consume a bunch of stuff and shit it out in a certain shape. The American economy is a digestive thing. Almost a peristalsis of I-work-and-then-I-consume-and-then-I-spit-out-and-then-I-consume-again. San Francisco—it's now the same.

It's this messianic tech thing. We're saving the world mostly making useless products that solve problems that real people don't have—it's problems that rich twenty-year-olds have. Like, "There's nobody at home to pick up the laundry that somebody else did for me." Thank God somebody is solving that, because what would we do otherwise?

You have an entire population of people who really haven't done a lot of humanistic learning. People who have been in science programs. Or engineering programs as undergrads, and so they maybe took one history class. And I think you can actually *feel* that. You can feel that in the callousness, in the oversimplification of political problems.

I am not in the trenches of the boom—living in a mansion with seventy-five other people, because it was cheaper to get than a San Francisco office, working on something that we think is going to change the world. I'm in a lumbering corporation that makes stuff very slowly and scoops up and consumes the little companies that show promise. I'm so insulated from any fluctuations that it's really hard for me to feel almost anything.

My job is to make things for people, and I can't do it. It's easier for me to understand a dolphin than it is to understand a person. Because my worst day is like, *The traffic was bad in my chauffeured bus. I had to sit in a comfortable seat with Wi-Fi for an extra twenty minutes.* That's the worst it gets.

I'm always composing my resignation letter in my head, that's what I do in the shower. It's always like, *Dear Larry and Sergey, I am leaving because this place is perfect. You guys have done such a good job of insulating us from anything that would introduce any worry into our lives that I literally cannot relate to a normal human being. Because I don't pay any of my bills, because I don't have to think about my rent. If it doubles, I don't care. Doesn't matter. You have completely turned me into a person who is incapable of doing his job.*

But one of the other consequences of living in a boomtown is that every time you feel like you have to leave—*I have fucking had it, I have absolutely had it!*—somebody comes over and is like, "Here's X amount of dollars," some ridiculous amount of money, "just because you're doing a great job. We love you!" Or, "Here's an email from the guy who invented the internet. Maybe you should stick around a little longer, maybe there's something you can do together."

As I'm getting older, I'd love to do something on my own. I have every confidence that I could figure something out. And I'd probably end up making lots of money and enjoying it. But at the same time, I'm too comfortable. I don't have to worry about anything, I don't have to think about anything. And without any struggle, it's very hard to find meaningful problems to solve.

Our obstacles here are mountains that we climb or waves that we surf. It's all about man versus nature. There's no man versus self here. And the man versus man, it's more like man stepping over man in the street.

Have you read *Mediated*? It's by Thomas de Zengotita. He talks about how when somebody says to you, "Well, this is reality . . ." that means, "You don't have a choice." So the opposite of "reality" is "optional." But here, all we have are options. You choose to care about this thing, you choose to care about that thing, you choose to cry about this thing, you choose to not care about that thing. We think life is about picking the "stuff," the information that affects you.

He talks about how disconcerting it is for many people to break down in the middle of nowhere, like Saskatchewan. All the rocks are in a particular place. The fences are somewhere, the telephone poles. But none of them were put there for *you*. None of them were put there to tell you anything. There is no interpretation. There is no message. You are stuck in the middle of nowhere, and nobody gives a fuck.

And that realization, that nobody has designed this experience for you—it's terrifying.

LESLIE DREYER

We meet near City Hall and I make a joke about the number of times she's probably protested outside this building. Part artist, part activist, she came to San Francisco to build a life with her partner. Then, the financial crisis hit in 2008, and the San Francisco housing crisis followed.

M*any of my friends were being evicted. Rents were skyrocketing.* Starting in 2010, 2011, it was just a huge upward curve. And at the same time, the Google buses were all over the streets, the program had really amplified in those two years. So that was on the tips of people's tongues. At every party: "Fucking Google buses." "Nobody else can pay rent except tech people."

I called the SFMTA to find out what law they were breaking: the curb priority law, which was a $271 fine every time somebody stops in a public bus stop without authorization. There's no enforcement, of course. So we were like, "If the city just fined them every time, then that would be . . ." And we calculated it: $271 times how many stops they did per day over the two years when the program had ramped up. It was $1 billion.

The buses represented a huge class divide—and the city privileging wealth, tech wealth. Since the corporate campuses are in Silicon Valley, the buses were the only visible symbol that we had access to. These corporations were not paying this fine. They were getting tax breaks on top of that. And our public infrastructure—public systems in general—were getting cut. There were Muni fare hikes. Rents were jacked up in the neighborhoods where the buses stop. Real-estate speculators and their agents were charging 20 percent or more around tech shuttle stops, which plays into who can afford to live here in the first place. So there's a link between tech wealth and evictions.

Why would you subsidize the richest companies in the world

and then make people who can barely afford to live here, who really need to use our infrastructure and public transit, people who live here and work here, pay for that subsidy?

Heart of the City Collective—that was what we called ourselves—we thought, *The problems are getting worse. We need to do something to "visibilize" this.* So we organized with a bunch of the housing groups and folks who had been evicted.

December 9, 2013, was the first blockade. We decided to "enforce the law." We wrote a fake ordinance from the "San Francisco Displacement and Neighborhood Impact Agency."

We surrounded the bus and had all the laws on hand, the state law that they were breaking, the local law they were breaking, the fine, and then the breakdown of the $1 billion in total fines and how it should be used for eviction defense and affordable housing and *yada, yada.*

We entered the bus in our fake city vests and we issued the ordinance. Meanwhile, people were surrounding it with street signs that said WARNING: TWO TIER SYSTEM and whatnot. We were careful not to block people from getting on and off.

A woman from the upper deck came down saying, "You're not allowed to be on this bus." I asked to see their permit to use the bus stop, and she said, "We're working that out with the city." Some other employee said, "No, no, no. Don't say anything." Because really they hadn't worked anything out yet.

We tried to have some conversations with tech folks there—I think those personal conversations are productive—but, you know, there's a lot of defensiveness. People felt vulnerable. We got the kind of typical response: "We didn't cause this. This is just our job." But they were all tweeting about it. It was all over Facebook and Twitter, which was funny. There were, like, a hundred-plus articles in one day.

Google issued a statement that was really benign. It said something to the effect that they were working with the city to do something about it. The mayor issued a statement, like, "Don't blame them." Very helpful. And the news was quick to sensa-tionalize it: "They just hate techies." I guess the us-versus-them story sells better.

We did it again a week or two later. And then again. It was very planned. Because they can reroute on a dime—text all the riders and say, "We'll pick up down the street."

We started timing them with hearings on the issue at City Hall. So we'd do a big blockade in the morning and then be like, "Everyone go to City Hall! Let's talk about this!" It was fun.

Immediately their supporters were quick to say it's "carpool-ing," it's cutting emissions. This was the justification used in the press and at City Hall. And you know, the numbers that they were crunching to justify subsidizing the Google buses—not one company tried to survey people who were displaced. People getting evicted every day that are driving for hours back to the city. So you can't say this is taking cars off the road. Actually, it's most likely putting more cars on the road.

The protests spread. Folks in Oakland started doing it, and different groups here in SF took it on. There were many block-ades over time. Some people took Google to court, and there was a long, drawn-out suit based on their not having to go through a review required by the California Environmental Quality Act.

But I think as a tactic, it sort of played itself out. We stopped six in a row timed with what was supposed to be the final hear-ing. Folks came back together to do that final one. The Last 3% was there to try to start making connections for the loss of the black population here.*

But people had grown used to it, and the media focus became

---

* The Last 3% organizes on behalf of the black community living in and displaced from San Francisco. In the 1970s, the black community made up approximately 13 percent of the city. That population shrank to around 6.5 per-cent in 2013, and then halved again by 2015—to around 3 percent.

too much about the buses themselves and not the larger systemic problem of inequality and displacement.

And now it's legalized. Recently, the SFMTA basically legalized the buses.

We were leaked the memo that Google sent to their employees to go testify at City Hall during the hearings about the tech shuttles. They gave them talking points: how much their community means to them, how they contribute, all the volunteer work they do. There've been moments we get some information that we can use. We gave the info to *TechCrunch* to expose that their so-called "community engagement" was scripted from the top. Eventually we tried to get the tech companies on board to defeat the Ellis Act.* Some of them did throw down, but I don't know how hard.

It's impossible to measure if they exerted legitimate pressure. These companies know how to use the language of helping the little guy, suggesting that they care. Google is a great example of such propaganda. They funded Free Muni for Youth for a few years, a $6.8 million "gift." Meanwhile, they dodged billions of dollars in taxes. This act is largely symbolic, and it's a fraction of what they should be doing.

People are used to making too much money and they don't feel a personal responsibility for what's happening. They could start an initiative with their coworkers for housing justice,

* A controversial state law that lets landlords evict residential tenants in order to remove their units from "rental use." Critics argue the measure allows landlords to bypass rent control and capitalize on the inflated housing market—selling the building, flipping the units into condominiums, or re-renting them at peak rents—while tenants relocate without proper notice or resources.

maybe consider giving away a huge portion of their income to mirror the median income of their neighbors. Because until you're on equal footing, you're not gonna experience what it's like to survive on what many of your neighbors make. So you're not incentivized to fight alongside them.

And because money controls the government, you start hearing people making excuses for this: "Don't we have the right to earn more money and send our kids to better schools? Because San Francisco's schools are just crumbling." That's where you go? You should have the right to send your kids to private schools because public programs have been defunded? Thanks, in part, to tax-dodging tech corporations? Instead of fighting for everyone to have the right to housing and education? One public school class in San Francisco had thirteen teachers in one school year, because teachers keep moving. They can't afford housing in the city.

Recently, the Board of Supervisors reclassified "affordable housing" to be for people earning 100 percent to 120 percent of the median income. That is no longer affordable; that's just a developer giveaway. But developers fund their campaigns. It's just this constant squeeze.

It's a global crisis. In Austin and Seattle—tech companies are growing there and a housing crisis along with it. Berlin and Barcelona and London and all these places are trying to deal with deregulated housing markets because of "home sharing" companies like Airbnb.

The Bay Area's history of resistance is helpful, but it seems the minute the movement gets in the way of capital, then it gets blocked or coopted. And it's hard to sustain the movement we need, when people are being displaced from their families, their networks. The support we need to do the long-haul work is being torn apart.

There's a blatant classism and racism underneath this history. White, wealthy folks are returning to cities because this is where the money is concentrated now, thanks to real-estate speculation and redevelopment schemes. People still blame poor people all the time—the myth of the poor person who's responsible for their own fate. *If they just worked harder . . .*

For everyone else, you pay rent or die.

Some of the stories tell the whole history of the city. The city has lost a huge percentage of its black population; the demographics of the Fillmore have completely changed. We had a big case: Iris Canada was a hundred-year-old being evicted from her apartment. Some of the owners wanted to evict her so they could condo-convert and make 40 percent more. They thought it was their right to have a higher return on their investment, of course. At the expense of a woman who'd been there since 1962. The last black woman in the building.

We did many demonstrations in front of the house. We did a big twenty-foot banner drop from the rooftop. We did a march through the Fillmore. We would show up at her court hearings and do demos outside of the courts. But we lost. She had two or three strokes because of all this.

After her eviction, she was in the intensive care unit for a month before she died.

They're continuing to cut funding for repairs in some of the last public housing that's left here. These are already practically slum shambles, mold, really dangerous living situations. Some of them are giant complexes, so that's thousands of people stranded in the only homes they can afford that are just rotting.

It's a systemic problem. And we have to have regional solutions, because no matter what we do in San Francisco, somebody gets displaced to Oakland, which has weaker renter protections. And then folks get pushed from Oakland to places like Martinez, which are further out and are really expensive already. And then, even if you find a place, you'll be kicked out the next year because there's no rent control in most of the surrounding cities. So that's why we have to look much broader.

People say, "Save this sector," or "Save the teacher," "Save the artist." But we need much broader legislation that's for all poor people. Because we shouldn't be competing or fighting each other for a basic necessity that we all need to survive.

This is the richest state. This is the richest *region* in the richest state. And we can't find a way to capture some of that wealth and spread it out? It's ridiculous.

MATT GONZALEZ

He got into politics because he was fed up. Working as a public defender, he had seen enough abuse in the criminal justice system, so he ran for district attorney. He didn't win, but the bid put him on the road to the Board of Supervisors, San Francisco's city council. He joined with a group of reformers and served from 2000 to 2005, the last two of those years as board president. Today, he is back in the Public Defender's Office, serving as chief attorney. His office walls are covered in works of abstract art, many painted by friends in the city.

I n the 1980s voters passed a ballot measure called Proposition M that capped how much office space could be built in San Francisco each year. It was promoted to stop the "Manhattanization" of San Francisco: that if we built too much office space, it might attract too many workers to compete for the available housing. And that could drive rents through the roof.

That's what the dot-com fight was about. Mayor Willie Brown, seeing an opportunity to attract business growth, got around the Prop-M limits by just decreeing a middle category. He renamed dot-com construction as something other than office space. The planning commission argued it was "research and development" space, so shouldn't be part of the growth limits. That was the first crunch: they allowed too much office space to be built, so there was insane competition for housing.

Activists flooded City Hall to urge compliance with Prop M. There were protests on a weekly basis, urging commissioners not to vote a certain way, asking the board to get involved. It was exciting, because you could see the opposition was real.

Fast-forward to now, and it's totally different. Because of Wi-Fi, tech workers can work down the peninsula yet live in San Francisco. They can board a bus and work during their commute each way. So you can't keep track of workers—for the purpose of calculating how much office space to build, how much housing is needed, how much tax revenue should be received. That's why everyone is confounded: this isn't happening within city jurisdictions anymore.

Suddenly you realize it's actually an indictment of municipal taxation. The whole idea of taxing a business located in your jurisdiction is to offset the impact of the workers on housing availability, transit, parks, other city services. Today, cities like Palo Alto and Menlo Park are collecting business taxes from tech companies headquartered there, but they aren't dealing with the impacts of the workers on housing. The link is ironic: the money to offset the housing crisis just isn't available.

The old rules are meaningless against the new technology—it allows these companies to pretend they are ungovernable. That's why everybody is confused. There are virtually no protests at City Hall because nothing is being voted on. The crisis isn't driven by decisions at City Hall or the planning commission. As things stand, City Hall is powerless to control it. And for the most part, the left can't even articulate what's going on.

Even the old powers that be—mostly conservative chamber of commerce businesses—have been damaged by the positions they took in the old political battles in the '80s and '90s. Many of them fought commercial rent control and now are being wiped out by tech companies that choose to headquarter here. They don't even get what happened to them, in the sense of being eaten up by their own choices. It's like one shark eating a smaller shark.

The whole problem cries out for regional taxation. But nobody knows how to do it. You typically vote within city boundaries where you also collect municipal taxes. Are we now going to be electing regional mayors? What would that look like? We have regional boards, but cities are at odds with one another: what we've lost, another city has gained.

It's slow. It's going to take time to sort out the new rules. And that's the thing about tech—they've benefited by the fact that government isn't agile enough to keep up with their blurring of the lines.

RON CONWAY

A San Francisco native, he made his start in computer hardware and software, but quickly realized his talents lay elsewhere. "I don't like managing people—this is why investing is perfect for me. I can go give five entrepreneurs advice, not get into day-to-day management, and watch them succeed." He made early investments in

Google, Facebook, Twitter, Pinterest, and on and on, becoming one of the industry's most prominent "angel" investors.

And he has done the same for local politicians. He was an influential donor to the past three San Francisco mayors. Like many Californians, he expresses passionate support for various liberal causes—gun control, open immigration, gender parity in the tech industry. And yet, he wrestles with the dissonance that plagues many of the area's most influential executives: Why does he face so much criticism from people to his political left?

'm speaking at the Crunchy Awards tonight. The Crunchies is a celebration, it's like the Oscars for tech. So, I can't go off berating people. I'm going to say the tech community has to take control of the problems in this city.

It's not just good-citizen stuff, it's about putting sweat into the city. You have to give up something. Government's not functioning, so you've got to jump in and do it yourself. It's just a philosophy I was born with. It's your duty to be civically engaged.

If you can't donate money, donate time. If you're not high-networth, fine, go out and do volunteer work. Get your company to adopt a school and volunteer in that school. That's the least you can do. Probably less than 5 percent of the tech workforce in San Francisco, around seventy thousand people, go out and do volunteer work once a week.

If you don't want to do that, then go do something else. Like Square: great example. Every Friday, they go out and pick up trash around their office. They weigh it. They compete with each other. They make it a game. They're all about getting clean streets around here.

San Francisco schools are getting better because Salesforce went in and adopted all the middle schools. That has given teachers all kinds of money to innovate. They gave every principal

$100,000 conditioned on the school district not telling them what to do with it, and you can't believe what these principals have done. You can even look at the test scores. Principals are comparing best practices. And that will spread to the rest of the city.

I started this group called One City because of the gentrification issue. Believe me, everyone in San Francisco knows about it. We're trying to say, *Hey, wait a minute, this is one city, let's all treat it like it's one city.* That's our new mantra. Tech people, and the people in Chinatown, and the progressives, and the haters—the ones who are stopping Google buses—all of us are *one.*

Because everyone says this new tech wave's another gold mine. This area is prone to gold. But this time, we can't let people make dough and leave.

We have such an opportunity with this new generation of tech kids. They're not computer-science engineers, they're designers. Designers don't want to live in the suburbs. These are people who want culture and art. They're artists themselves.

But the progressives of San Francisco have too much of a voice. These people are so unproductive. They don't want anything. They don't even want more housing, no more cars. They want a whole bunch of people to leave and make room for low-income people. They want the city to go backwards. And these are the super left-wingers who you would think would realize they are being pretty selfish. So I actually think it's really healthy if we shut them out.

This happened in the first bubble, in 1996. Silicon Valley was a bunch of semiconductor companies, computer companies, and software companies. Then along came Netscape, and it changed everything. The browser made the internet a commercial entity, and there was an explosion of internet software companies. All of the issues that we're having with gentrification now, we had back then. There were protests and everything back in '99 and 2000. Same types of protests, same aggression. The very same issues: cost of housing. "What are you doing, displacing us?" *Yada, yada, yada.*

I speak for the natives, and there're very few natives left. I was born in San Francisco. I love the city. I love the architecture, I love the bay, the hills, I love the views. It's not necessarily the people. I wouldn't want to advertise the city for its people.

One of the things that I deal with is just how busy some of these CEOs are getting. I was at a dinner just the other night, and I asked the guy if I could do my "One City" civic-responsibility pitch. And he said, "Sure, go ahead." But you could see some of their eyes glassing over.

Two of the guys came up to me afterwards and were describing catastrophic problems they were dealing with in their businesses. It occurred to me, these guys are so busy, this business is so volatile, things are changing so fast, they can't be expected to pay attention to this. They can't prioritize philanthropy.

One or two of them hire someone in HR who deals with community engagement, but that's a low man on the totem pole. He's not really able to get much leverage. It needs to come from leadership, it needs to come from CEOs.

I don't know how to solve that problem. We have a long way to go, which is why tonight I'll be harping on it again.

SAAD KHAN

He is part of a new generation of venture capitalists. He worked at some of Silicon Valley's most innovative firms and got to see how companies were built from the ground up. He was one of the first to invest in Kiva, Change.org, the SETI Institute, the Grow Local Project, ClassDojo, Upworthy, and IBM's Watson—tech projects tackling some of society's biggest challenges. His email signature reads, "Be Excellent to Each Other."

f you just read TechCrunch *all the time, you get the sense that money* is always flowing, and a billion dollars seems small. Watch *The Social Network,* and it's like this stuff is happening left and right. There's this narrative of a get-rich-quick story that is far from the actual truth. What's lost is that people suffered a lot of scars.

My old firm invested in a start-up called the Music Genome Project, back in the late '90s. It was started by a struggling composer who had been in Hollywood trying to do film stuff. He wanted to figure out a way to get personalized recommendations on songs based on his taste in music. That turned into a company called Savage Beast, a music-recommendation technology pointed towards business-to-business applications. But when all the e-commerce companies went away in the 2000s, post-bubble, these guys didn't really have much of a business model left. They pivoted again—not paying all their employees for two years—into something called Pandora. And Pandora became this internet music phenomenon. Fast-forward ten years, it became a multibillion-dollar personalized radio company, based here in Oakland. Of course, it took them over ten years to become an "overnight success." That guy had been doing it since the late '90s, and that's a long slog.

Now people find their way here who aren't in it because they love the technology. And they feel like they are entitled to a piece of the "future," this economy that other people created.

There's this feeling that if you're not nineteen and dropped out of college, if you're later on in your career, then you've already missed the boat. It's not really representative of how stuff actually happens. The data shows, it's actually the opposite. It's people in their forties who are really building a lot of the value. But that's not usually reported on.

Of course, the new generation is also super important for the economy here. But it's because people coming out of school will work 24/7. It's the engine on which a lot of the value is built, this incoming talent cycle. So it's important that they find it desirable to go and join these massive companies. It's all part of the ecosystem. The whole complex feels vertically integrated: someone finishes undergrad, they have a path, they go straight to a big company, graduate school, then a firm. These institutions keep them insulated from much of the world, and the next thing you know, they're a senior person in their field. They have resources. They have influence. But they've never actually worked outside of a pretty sheltered context.

Google is like Stanford. They recruit a lot from Stanford, but they also re-created a college campus. People are there late at night. There are beanbag rooms, there's Segways, there's free food—it's awesome. You can be there 24/7. They constructed an environment where people don't have to leave. I know a lot of people who went from Stanford straight to Google, spent seven, eight years at Google, so now twelve years of their life going through what feels like extended college.

And that's their whole career. They've done really well financially, so, *Hey, you must be doing something right*. They live this life going from Google to Facebook to Twitter to whatever. They hop around these really interesting companies doing cool stuff. But these environments are not representative of the rest of the world. And so they can end up with a skewed view of what the world looks like and what kind of problems they're really capable of solving.

Meanwhile, there's a much bigger structural shift happening in the labor market. It's going away from employment to this notion of liquefying work. The sharing economy: project-based, as-you-need-it stuff. Now, you can execute on your passions: you earn your income, in a flexible way, with a flexible schedule, so you can go work on the project that you're really excited about or bootstrap the business that you always wanted to start.

I take Lyft into work, and I've had some of the most amazing conversations on my morning commute: a Tibetan refugee, or an artist who's working on something on the side, or people building their own companies. I had the most interesting metaphysical conversations with a jazz musician who broke down what the world is all about. All in my fifteen minutes crossing the Bay Bridge in the morning.

The flip side is there's no job security. It's treacherous if you're looking for one career at one company. And the change is going to be very challenging for a certain class of people. I struggle with it a lot. I try to think about what's really going on here and does it make sense.

It's scary. It's also very different than the model before. My dad worked for one company in Silicon Valley for fifteen years. There's no analog for that anymore. Certainly not in tech. There's a different mind-set now. Even on the employee side, there is an ambition to do something that's more than a job. Part of it—if you take the cynical view—is instant gratification expressed in a career context.

We're also living in an ownership society where wealth accrues disproportionately to the owners. It's hard to understand how it got this way. The best explanation I can think of—and it's a stretch—is that people here place a huge premium on risk. Being the first person to get naked and jump out on that ledge. It's a lot more risky than being the fourth person. . . . This city was built off the back of treachery, the Traitorous Eight leaving National Semiconductor. The industry rewards risky behavior.

I guess it makes a certain kind of sense. All the great lessons come from failure. People don't learn a lot from success, they just know that it happened. But surviving is the biggest lesson.

LEON FIKIRI

He sits by the window of a café on Polk Street, between Nob Hill and the Tenderloin, looking down the street at an old strip club, now flanked by shops and restaurants, hipster barbers, all intended for the young professionals ambling by in the afternoon sun. Born and raised in the Democratic Republic of Congo, he moved here looking for opportunities, a better life. He had studied computer science, got a degree in networking systems. And he dreamed that he would be one of the young and lucky, strolling down this street in sunglasses and athletic wear.

didn't speak English at all. The first time I went to Starbucks—I had my dictionary with me, French-English—and I ordered a coffee. I was hoping the person would just say yes, and give me the coffee, and I'd pay and leave. But somehow, she asked me, "Do you need room for cream?" Based on the dictionary, "room" is a space that you find in an apartment, a house, something like that . . . So I learned to say no.

Or when I used to go to a burger place, and the person would go, "How do you like your meat to be cooked?" I go, "The way you like it." Sometimes I found someone who likes his burger rare, and it was very bad, or very well-done, but I had to deal with that. That's how survival instincts work.

I came here in 2008. The economy was going very bad. So I took the path that a lot of immigrants take. Work hard, work hard, work hard. I sold sunglasses. I was a waiter. There is nothing easy. You start working very early, and then you get to bed very late. You don't know any better. Just need to work hard. Many people went through even worse than me, and they kept going. They kept going, so I kept going.

It reminds me of that proverb—from Thomas Friedman's *The World Is Flat*. That every morning in Africa, the sun comes up, and a lion has to run faster than the slowest gazelle. Otherwise, he will starve to death. Every morning in Africa, a gazelle wakes up, and it knows that it must outrun the fastest lion. So it doesn't matter if you're a lion or gazelle in Africa. When the sun comes up, you better start running.

A friend of mine told me about Uber, "Why don't you try and see if you're gonna like it?"

I knew the city because, from time to time, I used to work with a limo service doing pickups for extra money. So I said, "Why not?"

It was about five years ago—the beginning of Uber. They had a small office on Ellis. I found, like, six kids trying to make it happen.

They were completely lost, didn't even know the city. They had a test, just one of the boys trying to ask me some sneaky ways around the city. He goes, "If you're taking Turk towards downtown . . ." And I go, "Turk is a one-way. It goes to the other side. Are you talking about Golden Gate?" He was trying to give me a test and didn't know the answers himself. He got lost between the Parc 55 and the Clift Hotel.

I was one of the earliest Uber drivers in the world. They learned from us, everything.

There was only one service at the time—black town cars, nothing else. Uber never advertised at the beginning. It's town cars who made Uber what it is now. We knew customer service. We knew how to build business long-term. Every client to us was an account.

It exploded. All of a sudden, everyone knew about Uber, everyone wanted to use Uber. Even that word became so popular that it became part of our language. It's like "Google." *I'm gonna Google it. I'm gonna Uber home.*

Uber gave me the opportunity to work, and the freedom of time. I worked twelve, fourteen hours a day, working hard to make it happen. I got my own car, and I got my own commercial registration, my own licenses, my own everything. I have my own company now, two other drivers, three cars.

They made a lot of promises to us, their "partners," that they want to help us. They're gonna make sure that if we invest money, we're gonna get a lot of money back. They used to send us text messages, "Can you please sign in? Because there is high demand."

But when you work with Uber, you have to understand that you're responsible for every single penny and expense. "We are middlemen. We connect you to the passenger. So you have to pay all your expenses, everything." They take a cut, first 20 percent, now 25.

You pay your own insurance. Besides that, you have maintenance. Especially in a city like San Francisco, with all hills. Can you imagine how many times I change the brakes, shocks, transmission? Cost me $8,000 once. You have to pay for gas.

When the gas hits the ceiling, here in San Francisco we start paying over four bucks. You have to pay your own health care.

All these expenses, they add up. At the end, you find yourself paying more than 50 percent of what you're making, just expenses. Just expenses!

Then they added UberX. So many people joined as drivers. They thought that UberX is the future. So they bought a car with a loan—they're paying a mortgage, they're paying a lot of fees—and they make almost what they could make if they work at Starbucks. The only difference is, at Starbucks, they will get health-care benefits.

But UberX drivers don't know where they're going. No training, no experience. They have no understanding of the city, no knowledge. Driving the wrong way on a one-way street, or driving completely wasted. I used UberX myself once. Someone tried to sell me weed.

San Francisco was a cake, and we used to be ten thousand people eating from that cake. Now we're up to a hundred thousand or more, eating from the same piece of cake.

Because Uber's goal is to cash out big money, big dollars, big bucks—make the maximum they can make. And, no, they don't care what they leave behind them. They don't care whether they have one driver or a hundred thousand, they just want a billion dollars.

I have nothing back home. One day, I went to my parents' house, and I found my mother lying on the ground. She had an aneurysm, multiple strokes.

Because my brothers were able to sustain financially everything medical, I felt like I had an obligation towards my mother, to take care of her. So I stayed with her at the house, twenty-four hours, seven days a week, trying to do all things, the bad things, the medicines, to take her to the doctors, everything. I did that for almost two years.

When she passed away, I buried her with my hands . . . I'm the one.

I took it as a failure towards life in general, because we didn't . . . we didn't have a lot of options. In San Francisco, for instance, she would have survived that thing. But the fact that we lived in a country so fucked up, so corrupted, with so many people living under a certain kind of political system that they learn how to be sneaky, to lie . . . They learn how to treat other people as animals and not as human beings.

I was in a kind of coma: my brain had stopped working, *I* stopped working. Nothing attached me there; I felt disconnected and unplugged. It's not worth living in a country where there is no future. That's not my home.

My sister was the one who told me about San Francisco. She owns a shop here. We were talking on the phone, and she goes, "Maybe if you come here, you will enjoy life again. Maybe you will live again. Maybe the flame will come back."

"So how do you like Uber?" We get this question a lot from people. I don't know why. We're not talking about cappuccino. "Do you like cappuccino?" It's like someone steps in your office, "How do you like working here?" And what, "A hundred percent, I love it. It's beautiful. It's amazing." That should be the answer?

Drivers, we talk about this. Some people, the first question is, "Where are you from?" One guy, he goes, "I'm from here." The lady, she goes, "You have an accent." He answered, "Because I drink a lot of coffee."

I told someone, "I was out of milk. That's why I moved here." The ride is only ten minutes, they want to have answers beyond their imagination. I should tell my life story between the Marina and North Beach?

It's arrogance more than ignorance. People nowadays see an Uber driver as an object. He has no value. He just comes with the service. Picks you up at the push of a button.

That's the sharing economy. They think they can use you as an object for a certain specific time—that they can do whatever they want with you. It's not sharing cars, it's sharing people.

One day maybe human beings will be obsolete. The self-driving car is almost done. It's not only drivers who will disappear. Brokers of insurance—who's gonna get insurance when no one is driving? Soon all the people who are so lazy they need a car to pick them up at the push of a button—all these people, they're gonna find themselves jobless too.

This is how it goes now. People don't value human beings; what matters is making money. Most of the time, the people I drive, they're not from here, and they weren't even here in 2008 when we had that crash. New people, they see San Francisco as a company. The city is a big Google: *I got hired, I'm gonna make some money. If I see another crash, I'm gonna move somewhere else.* Or the city is a mall: *I'm going to shop and leave.* What do they know? They don't care about the city. They have no respect for the people here.

I get so many complaints about homeless people. That never used to happen. But now they don't fit in people's image of the city. You don't like him sitting there or sleeping there? You think you should kick him out? He's a human being. He is not an object. He has the right to live. We cannot just take him in a garbage can and throw him somewhere else because you don't like it.

Try to do something about it. What about giving some time to read about why those people are there? Some people have issues. Some people were better than us, but they didn't have the luck. And our society here—I have to be honest with you—it doesn't give people the ability to restart from scratch, not like it used to.

At a certain time in my life, I almost committed suicide. If I had crystal meth, maybe I would have tried it. Maybe I could have been homeless now. There is a thin, very thin line between people who have a decent lifestyle and people who are on the street. Sometimes a matter of a fraction of a second.

I had this guy, a client. He got into the car. I can tell from his accent that he's from India, or Pakistan. No, no, don't get me wrong—no racism, nothing like that. It's just part of the story. He goes, "Do you like working with Uber?"

I said, "It's a trap. But I'm dealing with it. I'm doing it."

Then he goes, "Where are you from?"

"From Africa, from a country called Congo." I go, "What about you? Where are you from?"

He goes, "I'm from *here*." Just five minutes before, he told me he just moved here six months ago—but he feels, *I fit here, I'm part of this society.*

So he asks me, "You make money doing this?" I am silent. He asks, "So is it busy tonight?"

"It's Saturday night. Usually it's busy."

"So you're gonna make good money."

I turn around and go, "What is making good money for you?"

He says, "I mean, you're gonna make some good dough."

"No, no, no. For you. For *you*. What do *you* do for a living?"

"I work in finance."

"So how much money do you make?"

"I make, like, $200,000."

"So is that good money for you?"

He said, "Well, it's not bad."

"So I'm *not* gonna make $200,000. Do you think that you're

superior to me because you're gonna make $200,000? $200,000 is not good for me. Maybe that's what *you* think is good enough. For me, it's not, because some people are making $10 billion. Why shouldn't I be making $10 billion?"

He goes, "How do they make $10 billion?"

I told him, "Well, Picasso used to paint and make $15 million within five minutes. Why can't I? What separates me and you from him?"

The guy got frustrated and asked, "Can you please just drop me here?"

We get that more and more now.

I was here when Uber was at the beginning, when Travis Kalanick was at his beginning, or Brian Chesky from Airbnb, or Jack Dorsey was trying to make Square, and the beginning of Elon Musk doing Tesla.[*] I have driven many of them.

From my own experience, when you meet them, you don't see anything inspiring on them. You don't see that genius in them. These are normal people with regular IQs, maybe they're sneakier than others. Maybe they took the back roads, the shortcuts. In the end, I go to myself, *Well, it's a good thing, because it means it's easier to succeed in this city than it seems.*

But it's like these people sat down and fixed the next hundred years of what's gonna happen in the world. A new world order. Soon, we are going to share everything, own nothing. That's the new era, but is it healthy?

Because the sharing economy means we're gonna have less

---

[*] In June 2017, Travis Kalanick stepped down as CEO of Uber, forced out by investors after a series of scandals rocked the already controversial company.

control, less power to regulate it, less influence, less voice. Before we know it, we're gonna be Congo here. Where no one has influence, no one seeks justice. I left that mentality and mind-set only to find it here.

I've seen Uber treat people like shit. People begging for work. "Can you please let me begin?" "Please activate my card?" I've seen that before—begging, begging for work. The guy in front of them sits in a position of power—they start treating people like shit. People treated like shit because they don't know how to speak English correctly. For some, this is life or death. Absolutely—you work or you die.

I have seen this story already: a society that doesn't value human beings will end, just fail. People don't want to admit that we're not first in the world anymore. The Michael Jackson '80s is over. Maybe we have the best army in the world, the best economy, but for how long? What is the rating of our schools when it comes to math and physics, compared to other countries? Do I need to give my kids the same education I left behind in Congo? No. What about the employment rate? How many people that have access to health care?

I'm self-sufficient. I provide my own energy. But every time I meet with someone who's twenty-one, twenty-two years old, and he's telling me he's doing UberX full-time, I feel the obligation to tell him, "You're gonna be fucked. Go somewhere else. Build yourself a future. Go to France. Go to Europe. Go somewhere that will care for you. That will give you shelter, a justice system, education, medical care."

These are the difference between animals and human beings. I didn't get these where I grew up. I came here to find them, and I still don't have them.

The United States, America, is not a country. It's a corporation. It's a platform to make money. It's an app. Within that platform, you have the options of succeeding or failing. In both cases, you're responsible.

So you better start running . . .

I'm still running.

JAMES WILLIAMS

Growing up on a farm in the Central Valley, he had a lonely childhood, tending to pigs and vegetables, sneaking to the arcade and drinking tons of soda, dreaming of San Francisco. "You had to entertain yourself and find pleasure in solitary activities." So he became an artist, moved to the city, and opened a small studio in the Western Addition. Within a few years, the neighborhood got too expensive, the rent too steep, and he put San Francisco behind him.

Today, things have come full circle, and he manages a farm in Petaluma, north of the city. They provide a majority of the produce to Alice Waters's famed Berkeley restaurant, Chez Panisse, epicenter of the "slow food" movement. Together the restaurant and the farm preach the use of local foods and traditional production methods. The farm teaches aspiring farmers their craft: "We get people from all kinds of backgrounds. Hopefully go on and help people who legitimately need help."

When I got to San Francisco in 2006, with one of my best friends, we commented on how much we liked the city. Because it didn't seem like you had to be flashy and successful to have a good life. To have a rich community, a good lifestyle, a house. You could be a little rougher around the edges.

We were wrong. We were late to the show and just couldn't see the beginning of the deconstruction of possibility. Maybe I had an undiagnosed breakdown: working so much, teaching, bartending, doing freelance design work. I had a gallery that represented my paintings, but I was spread so thin, I wasn't making any progress. I just couldn't make it.

We were part of the initial move into this neighborhood, the Western Addition—now it's called "NoPa," North of the Panhandle. Then we watched two years of rapid change. And eventually, I had to leave. For financial reasons. I was part of gentrification and then suffered from it.

I feel a lot better about the way I spend my time now.

You're outdoors and doing things. It is stimulating and invigorating. And your body is all of a sudden activating in a weird way. I found my creative outlet is brightest when I am altering spaces. I am really into my garden, and I treat it like an installation piece.

Immediately, you're thinking about taking care of other people and being able to do that in the best way possible: by the way that you grow things, by the way that you treat your land, the way that you raise your food, the standards you use, the price that you're able to sell it to somebody, making sure that you're not excluding any community from what you've grown—these questions and concerns are built into the activity of growing food. What it means to have space and land, and how you use that to build community.

And working in an industry like this means you're inevitably working with people who don't have a lot of money. No matter their background or their race, nobody gets rich doing this. So you're already starting from a pretty good place.

Our head farmer has got this idea that if more people grow food on smaller scales for larger communities, little pockets of good nutrition, then everyone's brains will work better. It's funny listening to him talk about it, because he gets into the Cosmic Serpent big-time. The Universal Consciousness is blasting in his ear.

He doesn't have any idea how to talk to people, but he has this belief that nature is a little smarter than we are. You've just got to let it do its thing, help as much as you can without interfering too much.

Which means that there's tons of native weed and plant life surrounding everything—a mess compared to the row crop that you would normally be looking at. Those farmers look at his fields like, "Where the fuck is the food?" "Well, you have to dig around in it. The cabbage is in here." It winds up looking like a weird, pastoral, provincial field that just happens to have a bunch of kale in it.

There's a lot of reasons why it makes the food better, that have to do with soil growth, soil health, and maintaining a balance between how much you're partially disturbing, partially destroying the soil, and how much you're letting the plants take care of themselves and take up nutrients that they want. The surrounding plants also help with weathering, pests, erosion. When there's that much blanketed coverage and root structure, when it pours rain you're not going to lose anything.

For me, it is a more beautiful way of doing things. Philosophically and aesthetically. And I think I'm better at it than maybe visual art. There's also probably an untapped amount of information and emotion built from my childhood.

But there is also a culture surrounding the organic farm, this thing that does not attract certain parts of our community. A lot of it does have to do with prices. If you've got nothing but really expensive produce . . .

We live in the middle of an area that has got a huge Latino community, and I almost never see any coming in here to buy their vegetables. They get their vegetables at a local market with all the ingredients that they want, but not very good quality.

If you come here on a weekend, it's nothing but Audis and Lexuses up and down the lot. People that drive between wine country and Petaluma. I am always trying to figure out ways to get fewer Audis and Lexuses in our driveway, but I think there is just an invisible wall of like, "This cute little thing—this is for white people."

Land up in Sonoma County and in Marin, just because of its proximity to San Francisco—that's where a lot of this cost comes in too. There's only so many ways you can get around the sort of machine that is happening down there and changing things.

Two of our main farmers here are going to move to Wisconsin this year. They're going to be able to make as much food as they want, because they don't have the overhead of being in such close proximity to San Francisco.

Land prices, cost of living, a roof over your head. You have to be pretty creative living in an industry like this here. I built my own little house. It's right next to my garden. I spend almost no time indoors, in my living area. I just sleep there.

In two weeks I turn thirty-five. And often I think that if I did not work and live on this farm—I don't know if I could stay in this area. I would be homeless pretty quick for a little while, until I figured out what I was going to be doing next.

SAUL GRIFFITH

He was born and raised in Australia. His mother is an artist, his father was a textile engineer, and the family home was part studio, part workshop, part family hearth. They kept a large pad of cotton paper next to the telephone. Over the course of two weeks, Saul's mother's drawings of cupids and Rubenesque nudes would fill up his sister's landscapes, full of Saul's machines and buildings, surrounded by his father's math puzzles—layers upon layers. These notebooks captured the family in time and an alchemy that Saul would try to re-create as a husband, father, and engineer. He founded and runs a company called Otherlab, which designs moonshot technologies to protect the environment.

M*y wife, Arwen, and I bought this building, intending to have the* research side of our business and lab always be in this neighborhood that we liked. It was cheap. And this has been an industrial neighborhood for a hundred years, manufacturing.

So we're like, *Okay. We can have machines that manufacture and do industry here.* People didn't complain, because we did the thing that was always done here.

But now the people who work from home in the live-work lofts next door complain that they can't hear the sounds of themselves typing their 140 characters because of our machines in our industrial neighborhood. So fuck them.

If you invest, and you buy the building, and you're all in, and you're thinking about more than five to ten years—then you build gardens and you grow.

We put in all the plants on the sidewalk. We painted the murals on the walls. We upkeep the building as though we're invested in it for the long term. These aren't things that start-ups, or landlords with start-ups as tenants, give a fuck about.

I know every business owner by name in a two-block radius. So I know the people who own the art gallery across the road, the not-for-profit. I know the people at the wine bar and the guys who own the cocktail bar, and the chef who runs the two restaurants. We all talk to each other. We talk to each other about crime. We talk to each other about issues with the homeless people. That's how you build neighborhoods, with investment.

The problem with most start-ups is that they are set on a short trajectory—they are venture-funded and a number of the companies in the portfolio need to get exits within seven to ten years. "Exits" means they need an IPO or they need to get acquired, and you need enough of those exits to make your fund profitable. So they grow, and they move to somewhere else. They aren't really investing in the community around them because their tenancy in any building or space is one to two years.

It's the nature of modern work. It's inherent in the process of creating these new things that people have short tenures. These aren't companies just turning the sausage-grinding crank. The median person works for three to four years on any one thing, then moves on. In the software world, the turnover is two, or three, or four times faster, because there's such a huge failure rate.

We're the first generation that has had this at this extreme. I mean, we're all dealing with it. I've employed, directly, indirectly, maybe a thousand people since I moved to the Bay Area—smart, young people, best and brightest of every college, university. The only security you have now is to imagine with self-confidence that you can string together ten four-year gigs as a career. And if one of the gigs is really successful, it will become a ten-year gig, and then you'll get out.

We cannot socially continue down this path. I just can't figure out where everyone is going to be employed.

Look, I'm in technology, and I believe that we work on things that matter and count. But fundamentally what we do—everything we do—displaces jobs. It is the mandate of technology. You make things cheaper by eliminating labor. And we do that really fucking well. And I have no problem with that because I would like to eliminate some of my labor so that I have a three- or four-day workweek. I would fucking love that.

But what we have—at this pointy end of technology—is people working way too hard, way too much, not reaping any of the labor benefits. Even the people who are making the benefits that we should all reap collectively as a new Saturday, or something, they work harder than ever. A few schoolteachers and bus drivers may have the right workweek, but they are not earning enough and are rightly resentful.

So I only know two galleries of people: the overemployed and the underemployed. I don't know anyone with the right amount of employment that enables them to be civically engaged.

I am a father. I have two children. I used to think it was really important to raise our kids in the city, in a neighborhood that was a mixed neighborhood, where they would be exposed to all of the characters of life. But I've really become jaded, cynical.

We send our kids to public school. We volunteer an enormous amount. I teach science in my kids' class. All they need is inspiration, and that's easy to do.

The statistics in America show that the most money given is by the poorest people: it's equally true in terms of people giving their time. It's the poorest parents at the public schools that give the most time.

Two working parents who are commuting, spending nine or ten hours of the expected workday at Google and another two hours on the buses, barely making their rental payments, trying to raise a kid at private school because that's what they're told they've got to do—I don't think they have any time for volunteerism. I think they are a tax on the community. They take, take, take. They take all the good bits.

Then there's the homeless issue. People who obviously should be getting mental health care, or actually just plain old health care, if America, the richest country in the world, were able to provide it. Who instead are sleeping in tents in the cracks of my buildings. There is human feces in the garden that I planted to beautify our neighborhood, every morning—and the needles and used condoms and all the paraphernalia. Everything smells bad. Everything looks bad.

I've had visitors like Bill Gates come to my building—and the eleventh in line and the thirteenth in line to the US presidency, people who run things like the Department of Energy and people who are very high in the Department of Defense. "Would you mind stepping over this homeless person before I show you the future of technology?"

For the first few years you buy coffee, food for these people. Because you have sympathy. And you try to show your kids that you'll be nice. But eventually you can't deal with it anymore. I think my children sadly may just be observing me ignoring it and learning the cognitive dissonance that is required to live with it.

But we need to see more courage.

TIM DRAPER (CONT'D)

Not content with venture capital alone, he also has political ambitions. In recent years, he launched the "Six Californias" Campaign to divide California into multiple states. He wears a tie emblazoned with the movement's logo, a kind of primary-colors jigsaw of the state split six ways. If he succeeds, the fragments would create the per-capita wealthiest state in the nation, "Silicon Valley," and the poorest, the largely agricultural "Central California." Voters rejected his ballot initiative in 2014, but he is determined to push it forward.

look at California's government. We've gone from number one in educa-tion to number forty-seven. We dropped from the best place to do business to the worst. We now have four times the number of prisoners, and our recidivism rates are extraordinarily high. So by not educating, by making it hard to do business, we've created criminals. We have a real problem.

California is a monopoly supplier—such good weather, nobody wants to move. If you leave here, you lose the sunshine, the weather, the beauty, and you lose your friends. So, in my industry, what do we do to challenge monopolies? We start new businesses.

I thought, *Okay, I need to start a new state.* And the more I went down this track, the more I thought, *No, it's not fair to start just one new state, we need to start six, eight, ten.* Competition. Account-ability. It'll take a couple of years to get everybody's feet on the ground—but once you do, you'll have amazing governments. You'll see what each other is doing and improve on it.

So we started a ballot initiative.

In California, under the current regime, there are poor regions. They're poor because Sacramento has kept them stuck in this bad environment. Right now, the money comes from Sili-con Valley, it goes to Sacramento, but it doesn't find its way very easily back out. It doesn't find its way very easily down to the Central Valley or up to Jefferson. It's a shell game.

With six new Californias, imagine what could happen. It's not one restart, it's *six* restarts. You start from scratch, are you really going to start with the "dance of the lemons"? Bad teach-ers getting fired and showing up in the district next door? 1980s computers in the DMV and the election commission?

No, you're going to start fresh.[*]

---

[*] Tim got his initiative back on the ballot in 2018. This time, he is calling to break the state into three Californias, not six.

REGIS McKENNA (CONT'D)

He removes the silicon ingot from its acrylic case and hands it to me. It's cool—not as smooth as I expected—like putting your finger in dirt in the shade. He takes it back and begins to gesture with it as he speaks.

My father was born in 1898. When he was in his eighties, after my mom had died, he came out here. I took him around the Valley a little bit. He basically had worked his whole life in a public utility. I was showing him things, calculators, and computers, and he said, "I don't know how you're going to make it in this world. All these gadgets and so forth. This is really too much going on."

I said, "Dad, think about what you lived through. . . ." Electricity—I mean, he wired our original home, because it was all gas until then. The automobile. The airplane. Jet aircraft. Man on the moon. Television. I said, "How did you do it?"

You learn to learn and to adapt to your world. It's not even a conscious activity. It's just because you're interacting with the world all the time. As a child, it becomes more or less seamless. As an adult . . .

We don't know how to live in this kind of a world right now. I mean, look at the chaos! We're not making rational decisions. In fact, quite the opposite. This is what happens when people are not in *tune.*

It is this absorption of the technology without thought, because it becomes part of you very quickly. The iPhone became an extension of us. And literally people now, it's their ears; it's their eyes; it's their voice. It's everything. And somehow or other, we haven't put all the technology into any sort of a rational pattern as yet. We are still allowing it just to be absorbed without thought. Some people are trying to fight it, but it becomes very hard. And we're not capable of adapting fast enough.

This has been beginning since the '80s, with the start of the internet. I gave this presentation to a group of senators in Washington. I was very active in the New Democrats, Gary Hart was a close friend, Jerry Brown, Al Gore, and Bill Clinton, and so forth. I had a slide with two sides: one was black and one was white. And they were in a tug-of-war. I called one "matter," and one "antimatter." The struggle was between what matters and what is antimatter.

In the internet, there is no difference between the two. Because everybody has an opinion. Every time you say that something matters, there is an antimatter. And antimatter kills matter. They were predicting the world coming together—like the United States, Europe. And I said that we're going to see more disunity rather than unity. And technology has been a source of fragmentation.

Look at the infinite number of cars that are on the road. There may be all but a few manufacturers, but the cars all look different: different color, different shapes, different sizes, different stuff on the inside. And it happened in tech: software is infinitely programmable, infinitely changeable, infinitely adaptable. A computer can come out every twelve months and be completely new. And it's happening on the internet. Mass customization of ideas, beliefs, influence. That feeds into this feeling of individuality.

In my work, we did a lot of social-trends research. One trend they noted: Americans' "tolerance for chaos," they called it. For example, you can always put restaurant tables closer together. Americans will tolerate more noise, more chatter around them, and just sort of isolate themselves within it. We have come to accept a certain amount of chaos in our society. Traffic. Cost of housing. People are pushed out, but they commute here. They will tolerate the chaos of getting here. Look at history, look at Beijing, London. We will tolerate it.

Like the transistor. We are infinitely adaptable, infinitely programmable. But our lives keep getting smaller and smaller.

PART IV

THE
BREAKDOWN

ike any big American city, San Francisco has struggled with crime, with homelessness, with lagging public services. And as a region, the Bay Area got very good at sometimes hiding, even ignoring, those suffering most.

The area has weathered a rise in crime, especially street crime, property crime, thefts, robberies. Homelessness has surged, and many wealthy suburbs are overcome by this problem for the first time. Cities are declaring bankruptcy, schools are failing students, hospitals and clinics are struggling to keep up. California's prisons were so overcrowded that the Supreme Court ordered the release of thousands, citing cruel and unusual punishment prohibited by the Eighth Amendment. Each of these symptoms describes a disease that attacks the cities' most vulnerable: the young, the old, the sick, the mentally ill.

Perhaps most distressing, the civic immune system that we depend on is in its own struggle for survival. Many teachers cannot afford to live near their students, doctors near their patients.

Nonprofits cannot keep an office near the communities they serve. The problem is bigger than public servants and their commutes. It is about a void of expertise that is expanding with each departure, those who had dedicated themselves to standing on the front lines leaving their watch, and the community unable to see and respond to the crisis as it evolves.

TITUS BELL

Twenty-two years old, he lives in the Tenderloin. After his father passed away he was put in foster care until he aged out of the system. He crashed with friends, girlfriends, family, trying to keep off the streets. A tattoo on his arm names a nearby housing project: "That's the neighborhood where I was doing most of my dirt. I had done a lot of things there to prove my loyalty."

The reason why people came here, for the gold, is the same reason why people still come here. It's still gold here.

But it is rare to find people who succeed in my spot, because the system isn't designed that way. You go to jail and you get sent out, back to the same environment, same resources, and you're expected to magically find a way to get through all the crap. A majority of people right back in prison in like three months! That makes no sense. It's a setup for failure. Even though you get released from jail, you're *still* in jail.

The Tenderloin, it's disgusting. You could literally walk down the street and there's a dude just shooting up right there. Or the

Muni station underground, dudes shooting up. You're like, *Oh my God!* People just defecating everywhere. It smells horrible.

I've always wanted to live somewhere else, where it's nice and cool and relaxing. And your own people not wanting the same thing, you're just like, *Dude, how the hell am I supposed to do this by myself?* It's a lot of sacrifice, hella hard, because you need help. But your own people want to hold you back. Sometimes the family puts this guilt on you. Like, "Oh, you don't love us? You don't want to help us out? Well, forget you."

I understand why my dad acted the way he acted. The influence of the environment you live in—the Tenderloin. And coming from where he come from. He started on Oxy, then was hooked on heroin.

The system dehumanizes people of color, poor communities. *These people, they're lazy.* That's the dehumanization. *They don't want the same things I want. They don't want to put in as much work. They're victims, so they think like victims.* And so they make sure we stay victims.

Think of prison labor: so many companies get their products made in prison. It's much cheaper. These men get paid ten cents! That's exploitation. It's a new system of slavery.

You think about slavery—they demanded more slaves because they demanded more product. Product is king. Either you're making the product, selling the product, or you're in everybody's way.

It makes it easier to kick people out. *Oh, I'm about to go to this area and open up a Google.* The majority of the stores on Market Street, black-owned, neighborhood places, have been bought out by coffee shops, bike shops. And they don't hire the people from the neighborhood.

They're about to open up a new bank on the corner of my street. They're building this new, nice-looking mall, but there's this homeless person sleeping right outside of it. That makes no sense to me! I don't get that.

It's hard to explain, it's hella hard to explain. How dehumanizing it is. How exploited I feel. Because the city does not help the poor at all. And when these companies come in they say, "We *need* this. This is gonna raise the economy up. So we won't care what happens to these people. They need to move out!" And they're like, "We're not going to help you get housing. You have to figure that out on your own. It's not my fault that you didn't do the work to find resources for yourself. So, sorry."

And the recession made it worse, everything went crazy! When you affect the family's income, everything changes. Everything. Longer hours. Longer hours cuts that quality time, you know, the family dinnertime talk. So what happens? You spoil them. *I'm gonna give this kid everything that I didn't have. Here's a phone. Here's some Jordans.*

Kids start thinking things. Kids need that attention. Kids who say, "I put all my worth in these shoes, and if you mess up these shoes, I'm gonna smoke you." They start believing that they have to take care of themselves. Kids who say, "My mom don't take care of me. I have to worry for myself." You're only twelve years old!

After eviction, a lot of people go to homeless shelters, family houses. A two-bedroom for a family of five. Kids who couch-hop. There was a lot of that, hell yeah.

At that point, you try to get some love out in the street from friends who are going through the same thing. And the self-medication—smoking, drinking—it's all to numb it, just to get through it. But it's really self-destructive.

So, everything that I went through was kind of what was happening globally around me. I lived it and I seen it. A lot of my friends were getting smoked, getting killed. Over petty stuff. You're not even thinking about your future. Because when you're a kid, right, and you get evicted or you're homeless now—how are you gonna make money? You sell drugs. *Product is king.*

When your friends pull up with $900—ha, in one day!—whatcha gonna do? You're not about to work, what, how many hours? You're gonna *pick, pick* that money.

And it's easy too. And that's the thing. It's so easy. It's simple. Anyone can literally go out into the street and make a profit. If you know what you're doing.

I got those Oxy pills from my dad, and was like, *Oh my God. I'm good at this. I know how to demand a product and resell it for more than what it's worth. Hell yeah.*

And you have family in the street. Family, where everything is balanced, there's not too much worries, and you know someone is gonna have your back without even having to ask for it.

That's why it's insidious. It feels good at that moment. Because you're getting recognized. It was worth it, yeah, to get that love back.

It's a different world. For some folks, you pull an all-nighter and you get that A on your next test, your family is gonna be like, "Good job!" For us, you make a lot of money and you risk your life for it, "Bro, you sick! I need to rock with you!" You be like, "For sure!" You feel like, *Hell yeah. I'm the one. I'm the man!* Same thing, different circumstances.

No one's offering us anything else that gives that same feeling. Because this is where the gold is at.

AMANDA MACHADO

Something about her own education made her want to be a teacher: coming from a good high school, being the first in her family to go to an Ivy League college, and nonetheless feeling always a little behind her classmates, always somehow struggling to catch up. "Seeing all these other students that had come from such different backgrounds—and a lot of ways, more privileged backgrounds, boarding schools and things like that—just made me realize this stark difference in what kinds of educations and experiences people get, depending on where you grew up or how much money you have or what school you end up enrolling in." She spent several years teaching high school English in an Oakland suburb.

K ids, they're honest. They'll say something so jarring that you just can't get it out of your head. "I don't listen to you because you're not black. If you were black, I would listen to you because my mom is black. I only listen to black women."

Or the Latino kids saying, "I don't want to learn English because English is a white-people thing, and my family's not white. And I don't want to be like white people." Or telling me, "You don't really talk Latino," or "Your Spanish isn't that great, you're not really Latina," or "You're from Florida, so you're not actually Latina."

You just want to teach verbs, but Katie can't sit with Antonio because Katie's Hispanic and she doesn't like Antonio because Antonio is from El Salvador, or he said something about her mom the other day. Or the kids from East Oakland hate the kids from Hayward, and the Hayward kids hate the Asian kids, and the Asian kids hate the black kids. You think you're just going to pair kids off for an English assignment, but really, there's a war going on in your classroom.

A lot of single parents, a lot of abusive fathers, a lot of alcoholic fathers, alcoholic mothers, drug abuse, a lot of gangs in their neighborhood, a lot of police brutality. The Oscar Grant case was going on, and a lot of my students were really angry about that.* I remember one student came in telling me that his cousin just got shot by the police. So that was very real for them. A lot of them in Oakland would deal with their apartment getting robbed or violent things happening near their house. Put that on top of what you normally want to be dramatic about as a teenager, and then it just becomes too much.

A lot of the issues were just low-income families struggling with money. Your mom comes home a little late every day because she works so much, so she's not reading to you, and she probably doesn't take you to all these extracurricular activities that enhance your ability to learn or to experience new things—then you're going to be a little behind. Even if your mom and dad are very caring, the simple fact that they don't speak English, they don't have college degrees, and they come home late every day, and you have to take care of your siblings while you're doing your homework—that could make a huge impact on how you end up doing in school.

There was a student from Burma who had just gotten here, his English was nonexistent—I was concerned about him, and wanted to meet his parents. I knew they didn't speak English either, but I was excited to make them feel welcome. Instead, he came in with a "guardian." Since they were refugees, his family was assigned a person from the United States to help navigate things.

She was a white American from Oakland. He seemed really uncomfortable to have her next to him. But she seemed like a very nice lady and was trying to explain to me what he goes

* On January 1, 2009, at the Fruitvale BART Station, Oscar Grant was handcuffed by the police, forced to lie facedown, and was shot in the back. His death sparked protests throughout the Bay Area, anticipating the Black Lives Matter movement.

through every day. I conducted the conference the way I would with any parent.

But then she told me that the family had just gotten robbed, everything stolen, the kids and the family at gunpoint. That's part of the reason why the parents weren't there. They're struggling with that, trying to move to a new neighborhood that's safer. And I felt incredibly naïve.

There's a lot of good work being done. A lot of the nonprofits in the Bay Area are tackling the problem in interesting ways. And I think a lot of charters are getting good results and sending kids to great schools. That's amazing, but is that really all we need to be doing? Just helping some students escape their community by going to a great school?

The more difficult—but I think worthy—goal is how are these students going to end up becoming really *good people, good citizens* that are going to eventually come back and help their community? Or help another community? Or just be mindful and aware of how this whole thing works?

I related to the high-achieving students, the nerdy kids, the straight-A students, the quiet ones in the back, just trying to study and get into a good school. That was who I was, so that made a lot of sense to me.

I struggled with the kids that were rebellious or just weren't taking that approach. And they struggled with me. With such big classes, they don't get support, so it becomes virtually impossible for them to plow through when they have all these other things going on. They are slipping through the cracks.

There's a lot of talk now, especially in California, how the suburbs are now poor areas. Because Oakland's getting so expensive, and San Francisco is, of course, *really* expensive. At twenty-two, it didn't make any sense to me that I was teaching in a suburb with a bunch of kids that were from disadvantaged backgrounds.

But, gosh, a lot of my kids never have been to San Francisco. Their life is so removed from that. They would joke: San Francisco is a "white-people city" or a "rich-people city." It didn't play into their daily experience. It's far. You have to go forty-five minutes on the bus. Sometimes it feels like you'll never get out.

TONY SAGRADO

His work as an advocate for kids facing incarceration has been recognized by the governor of California and the attorney general of the United States. He has changed lives and changed how California, even the country, approaches juvenile justice. We are squatting between cardboard boxes in the back storeroom of the nonprofit where he works, an organization dedicated to helping kids avoid incarceration and remain at home, in their community. He offers me the only cushioned chair and sits on a plastic one himself.

remember saying, "I'm going to attend every funeral."

The way some of these communities grieve, it was foreign, really foreign to me. They have the SWAT team outside, patrol cars cruising around the block. Because this kid was shot in a drive-by, there's the potential for retaliation. Or they have the whole gang there, so their rivals may think, *Why don't we just light up the whole funeral home or the whole church?*

Three-hour-long funerals. Open mics. I'd never been to a funeral where they had open mics.

Now, on a semiregular basis, I look down at kids in coffins.

———

When I was in college, I worked at a grocery store. I worked the swing shift at night, and we'd take our breaks out in front.

One night, these two kids come by on bicycles, and they fall off right in front of us. One of the kids says, "They were shooting at us with a BB gun." The other was bleeding and bleeding from his leg. I looked, and it was a bullet hole. Through-and-through bullet hole in his leg.

He fell, we lifted up his shirt, and he had three bullet holes in his back. He was struggling, breathing. We called 911. I held his hand. He died on the way to the hospital. I found out when the local newspaper called. I saved the article.

So when I started doing this work, it really clicked for me. There's moments you feel like you're just right in your own wheelhouse, like you have the tools and the gifts to do well.

A kid is charged with a crime, and he's placed in juvenile hall awaiting trial. There's a bunch of research on how custody leads to further criminal activity—and the thought is that you divert this kid from spending unnecessary amounts of time in custody, you save him from the cycle of crime. So we argue for them to await trial at home.

We say, "If you let this child out, we will make curfew calls every day to make sure they're home. We will do school visits to make sure they're going to school. We will be in contact with their probation officer, with their family."

And man, I felt like I was fully alive when I was doing it. You stand up and you put your name on the line, *I'm responsible for this child*. Basically, we offer ourselves. Our word.

My first case was this young kid. He was living on Treasure Island. I looked at his school record, and he had missed not days, not months—he had missed *years* of school. His mother was a crack addict, but she was the sweetest woman you'll ever meet.

I remember meeting them at their home. I'd never been in a home like this. These smells I've never smelled before. Have you ever smelled crack, what it smells like when it's being burnt? That smell, I'll never forget that smell.

The floor was carpet, real thin, worn spots where you can see the concrete. There was no pad or anything. It was very cold and dank. It felt like the outside on the inside. That's the only way I can describe it—it just felt like the outside. No warmth that you would expect from a home.

But his mother, she cooked me a meal. I'm looking at that kitchen—I'm not a germophobe or anything like that—but the kitchen and the pots and pans, they just looked filthy. I thought it must have been a haven for mice and roaches. And I'm processing all this while she's making fried chicken and collard greens there on the stove. And I'm already committed. I know I'm going to eat this meal.

I look back and really connect that with my faith. That family didn't have much to offer me; they did what they could. They were warm and welcoming in an unwarm and unwelcoming place.

I saw myself in her. How much of life is trying to put something together, put the pieces back together, and to be accepted or to be loved?

I really connected with them. The father was eighty years old, there was a huge generational gap. She smoked crack and drank probably every day—the kids had to watch that—but she was there in every meeting. Intoxicated, but she loved her kids.

He started attending school twice a week. The probation officer was like, "We need to lock him up. We *need* to. He's only going two days a week. *Blah, blah, blah.*"

I stood up in court and I had his previous attendance records. A's on the whole thing for months and months of absences, maybe a spotty P here and there for present. And I was like, "Your Honor, I understand the court's concern, but you've seen how far he's come . . ." She was soft on him, she threw some grace his way. And that kid ended up doing really well.

I have never worked with a kid that I didn't think could make it. Not all of them, obviously, do. The problems are complex. Each case is unique. But bureaucracies don't know how to treat people as individuals. Their approach is very one-size-fits-all. And as a result, the system is a huge net. Once you're caught it's hard to crawl out.

We had this one girl. She was about four feet tall. She was a lesbian girl, very strong, a stud. Everyone was scared of her. She had a lot of sexual trauma in her past. She caught a case for robbery, ended up in the system, and just kept failing probation. Kept getting violated, kept doing time, eventually ended up in a group home. Failed that too.

We got working with her. By then, she was seventeen, eighteen. She might've had twentysomething school credits, not a lot at all. Which was one of the reasons why she always failed probation. You've got to attend school regularly.

Sitting in a school meeting, she totally has this breakdown. She's crying tears and she comes around to it: turns out she has a learning disability. No one had ever evaluated her. Because we miss her learning disability, she never comes to school, lands on the street, becomes a troublemaker, smokes, and goes to jail . . . And that's how it goes.

And it was relatively a minor fix. In a matter of a week, we plugged her into the right classes, and she was thriving. Her judge actually came to her graduation. We were all there. All cheering her on. She's one of those kids—no one would have batted an eye if she had been forgotten—but suddenly someone's paying closer attention.

Sometimes I feel like we're not even a drop in the ocean. This thing is so big. We're never going to win. And at the funerals, the hopelessness really hits home. Parents aren't supposed to bury their kids like that.

But I tell myself, *I'm not going to quit.* We can be more flexible. We can find gaps in the system. Looking at each kid, finding those areas where they have need and pouring ourselves into helping them, it's funny how simple the change can be.

Working in nonprofits, the pay is not that good. My buddies, a lot of them are either in tech or are bankers, attorneys, and whatnot. Several times, I've been so embarrassed that I've lied about how much I make . . . just in the spur of the moment. I don't make much money. And the benefits—I work for a small organization, so any family member, it's really expensive to add them. And my wife stopped working after we had our daughter.

She came real early—twenty-eight weeks into the pregnancy. Two pounds five ounces. She didn't cry.

This is her. [*He shows a picture.*] She was about the size of my hand. A little peanut. [*He shows another.*] This is her a couple of months along. They saved her. She spent her first five months in the NICU. That was two years ago. She ended up pulling through. But she has some difficulties.

After that, we realized that doing the work of my heart, it's not going to pay the bills. I have this baby in the NICU—my wife's benefits are about to run out. And I've got to get another job. Just for the benefits. In her first year, all her bills were like a million dollars. She's since had some surgeries, so she's like the $3 million baby.

So a job opened up to work for the city in Juvenile Hall. To be a jail guard there. They call it the baby penitentiary. I put in for it because . . . well, really competitive city jobs pay well, and have great benefits.

Now I'm a walking contradiction. My day job is here—working and advocating for kids. And then, at night, I'm a guard. For the last seven, eight years, I have been advocating for kids, telling judges that we don't fix society by incarcerating them: "It's treatment, it's services, it's interventions, it's . . ." And at night, I work in an institution that is part of the problem I try to fix during the day.

My first or second day on the job, and I'm doing these fifteen-minute room checks. Late at night. Each kid has their own room, and the rooms have these little windows. They become these depressing cabinets. I'm looking into these windows at these kids, kids that I'm fighting for in my day job. And I'm about to cry.

I'm trying to think economically, *It's just another job.* But if they see me crying, I'm never going to . . . It's a kind of betrayal.

It was hard telling people that I took this job. One of my closest friends, she's a public defender, one of the best in the city. And I waited the longest time to tell her. Because I was so scared. She's my hero. She had known about my daughter, she had been through that with me and she knew the financial struggles . . . And we were sitting in her office and she was just like, "I understand."

I soften that blow, trying to think, *I am going to be the good one. I'm learning a lot. Wherever the path is taking me, I'm going to look back and value this time. This is just making me a better person. I'm going to be the best guard. I'm going to be a change agent. I'm just undercover here.* I guess the talk is I'm the softest guy in there. I sneak chips in and different things like that. It's a way of connecting.

But I found out very quickly that the culture is overwhelming. My colleagues are very tough on the kids. Very. They have that whole mentality: "We *slam* kids." I've seen stuff in my short time . . . I've seen stuff in there that . . . it's some serious shit. And it's regular. It's the norm and my . . . the lines are so blurry for me . . . This shit we're doing, it's not right.

And I want to believe that it won't change me. But if I'm there long enough, it will. You're seeing kids in detention. What that does to someone's psyche. Just even the little things of slamming a door on a kid, hearing them throw up, putting kids in shackles and cuffs, restraining a kid.

I put a shirt on with a shield, a star, and I feel the dehumanizing effects of the uniform. Outside, I can wear whatever I want. There, I got to wear these big, baggy, black cargo pants, and I've got to wear these shoes. The architecture and the aesthetics of the pen, it's just very cold.

But quitting means moving. That's the thing: I'm deeply connected to the families I serve during the day. This is my heart. This is the community I surround myself with, I want to be buried here. I don't know anywhere else really. Where would I go?

I want to tell myself I have an out. This is just a means to an end. I'm not going to be this guy for twenty, thirty years. I'm here for a couple of years only. Then, when my daughter's a little better, my wife starts working again, I won't have to work this second job. I tell myself that—that's me just trying to get by—I *won't be there that long.*

But I've got to be there Monday.

CHRISTIAN CALINSKY

He stands outside his shop on Haight Street like a friendly neighborhood guardian. The area was once famous for being the heart of the counterculture. And it has always attracted the young and the lost looking for some of that old hippie magic. He was no different and had spent years living on the street, in and out of recovery and in and out of prison. Today, he's like a reverse Fagin, coaching his young "outside neighbors," helping them clean up the neighborhood, themselves, and get off the street.

met this girl named Misha and she said, "Let's go to San Francisco." And I was like, "All right."

I called my grandmother. She would help me, still, if I was in desperate need. I'm like, "It is raining nonstop and I can't sleep outside. I need to get somewhere else." So I ended up here in '96, got off the Greyhound, and went straight to Mission and Sixteenth.

This was before Care Not Cash,* so you could come to San Francisco and get a wad full of money and a free hotel, the junkie's dream. Hundred forty-seven dollars cash, plus a hotel room for three weeks—emergency housing.

Misha went down to do that because she had ID. And when she got back she's like, "I'm gay. I want nothing to do with you. I hate men. Get the fuck out."

"What? How did this even happen? You liked me a few hours ago . . . in a way that made me think that you were not . . . that you're at least *queer!*" So my first experience in San Francisco was Mission and Sixteenth, homeless and getting duped by a woman.

* A measure passed in 2002, sponsored by then Mayor Gavin Newsom, that cut direct cash assistance to the homeless in favor of funding shelters and other programs.

A girl named Kristine said, "You don't want to hang out here at night." So I came up to the Haight.

Golden Gate Park nearby has been a draw for a hundred years. Even during the Gold Rush, this park was like a campsite, basically. Then the hobos started coming. Then the hippies came. And now the street kids are living there.

It's a different demographic, sort of the elite of the homeless. You're not so bad. You're not so strung out that you're having to hook or break into cars. You're not having to do the things that most of the people in the Tenderloin are doing.

And Haight Street kids know it. "We're Haight Street kids so we're better off. We're still viable humans." Or, "I'm not in the Mission because when I'm in the Mission and dabble with those drugs . . ." Or, "At least I'm not in the TL." It's this whole privileged class inside the homeless population.

But the longer you stay out there, the more likely you're going to end up in the TL. That's all I got to say about that. You become clean, business-professional, dead, or a junkie in the TL. That's the choice you face.

Back then, your groups would "take out the trash." They would kick out anyone not behaving a certain way. "You can't be on Haight anymore." And if you didn't leave, they'd *pond* you, put you in Hep C Pond, used to be full of needles. They'd just throw you in the lake and you're guaranteed to get stabbed.

I was on and off the streets for years. When you're living outside, you're basically feral. And I had a hard time getting un-feral. You have a certain way of living, and then you get indoors and you're like, *I don't know how.* . . . They put you in your spot, and you've got to keep all your stuff in a neat little corner.

I was very good at finding people to fix me, I did that my whole life. One of the girls that I was having sex with got pregnant. I was like, "Okay, well, I love you . . . I love you, right?" Because I know what love is. We get married. She's the One, the Fix-All. I have three kids with her.

I got clean in 2000 for three and a half years—and then relapsed and relapsed and relapsed. I got clean, and got arrested for direct sales of heroin and coke. In San Francisco, that's not a big deal. They always let me out that day.

But then I'd get out and I'd go to the TL, and I'd shoot heroin and smoke crack, and I'd be back, same place I was eight months prior, in a couple of days.

One day, my wife had enough. She went to one of my best friends and was like, "I'm done. I'm done with him. I want him to say goodbye to his kids. I don't want them asking questions anymore. I want them to see him in his worst environment."

I was in the TL at the time. They paid a drug dealer to go find me. The drug dealer dragged me downstairs—he actually had me in a headlock. And there's my wife, my best friend, and my two kids at the time. And I weigh one hundred twenty pounds, I'm strung out, I stink, I have a string tying on size thirty-two jeans. Total wreck, one hundred forty pounds lighter than I am now.

She's like, "I've got $200. We're going to get a hotel room. I'm going to give you a weekend with your kids so you could say goodbye." With that money, I went and bought a bunch of heroin, went to the hotel, spent most of my time in the bathroom fixing.

My kids, they had no idea . . . I mean . . . no idea what was going on with me. They just knew that I looked like a skeleton. They kept saying, "We love you," one of them kept asking, "Are you sick? Why are you sick?" I was like, *Okay, I'm going to go get high.*

And then I got arrested. That night, January nineteenth, was the last day I used. That was 2009. Since then I've been clean.

Until now, the people of San Francisco have been the counter-culture. We're all fucking weird, and we fit in here—there was a certain calling that made us feel comfortable. The homeless kids also latched on to that. We found family here for those of us who didn't have one.

There's a whole different genre of homelessness now. I see a lot of families living in their cars. With half of their belongings on the sidewalk. And they can't afford to live anywhere. The crisis is becoming more visible now. The contrast is getting darker.

The people moving into the Haight now are first year out of college, working down in Silicon Valley. And they're like, "Oh my God. There's a homeless dog with his owner." Some of them try to make me out to be the bad guy, for taking care of these kids. Like I'm making homelessness okay. But I'm just trying to fix what other people broke.

These kids are just your outside neighbors. They live outside. Most of them will clean up after themselves, most of them will be respectful of where you live and move. They're neighbors. They just can't afford to live in that $4 million house.

MAYA WILLIAMS

Her mother was a doctor, so she practically grew up in a city hospital: "It's just shaped me. I like the hospital smell, that clean smell. That's actually a very calming smell to me. It tells me this is a clean situation, it's safe. When you're a doctor's kid, none of this stuff is traumatic." Today, she works in one of San Francisco's busiest emergency rooms.

The ER and the DMV are places no one can escape. You're going to be sitting next to whatever your town looks like, and it looks back at you, right in the face.

You get very affluent people and homeless people and everything in between. I could take care of the mayor and, the next minute, that thirtysomething, wealthy, unclear-what-you-do-for-work young person. The young professional who just moved into the area for some random thing, then resuscitate some homeless guy who overdosed on heroin.

I'm a public-health person too, so I think of people more as a population. That's why it's important doctors have a stake in the community: I live where I work. Here, there's a lot of homelessness. A lot of unaddressed mental illness, drugs.

You can displace all the people who have enough resources to move away and survive. But what do you do with the people who are like, "I'm so poor that I can't even buy a car, which means I have to live in the metropolitan area, and work, and I get paid cash in three different jobs under the table, and there's ten people living in my house." It's hard to get rid of those people.

Even harder to get rid of the homeless, the mentally ill, where are they going to go? Then you start to see a huge gap. All these affluent people who are able to afford to live in this crazy place juxtaposed with the destitute who can't afford to go anywhere else.

If you see a homeless person, you probably don't know how they got to that point. I get all-access, because it's all relevant. "Why" is the best question. If someone's in the ER because their heart failure is out of control, they missed their medication, you never know what's going on until they tell you. "I can't afford it." Or, "My wife died last month." Or, "I'm homeless, and my bag got stolen."

I see people on their worst day. And the worst is so relative. You dropped a wineglass on your foot, or your heart is failing.

You realize just how resilient people are and resourceful. And it does start to give you some perspective.

You see the impact of gentrification on people who take care of their parents or family members that are ill, parents taking care of small children with nothing—who live in their car, but their kid is still clean and going to school. And you think to yourself, *I barely get up and get my cup of coffee in, barely get here on time in my car that was fully gassed.*

Or mentally ill people with schizophrenia who come to the hospital, they're actually taking their medications, they're afraid because the voices are back. You see those sorts of things, and you don't think you could handle it. But you see that people rise to the occasion. The majority of people rise up to the occasion, no matter their station in life.

It's actually the minority of people who are addicted to drugs and *can't* get it together and *don't* take their medicines—a small chunk of the population that drive lots of the public costs.

You never want to see the same people over and over again in the ER, because then you know that the system is failing them. We're the last resort—the safety net, we're always there. If you can't get in anywhere else—a doctor, a specialist, a clinic—you come to the ER. So when you see people continuously, you know that they are not plugged in: they should have a primary care doctor, or a specialist, or whatever to help with their needs.

Access, money, education, mental illness, behavior problems, addiction. If you don't have a stable place to live or, say, you have to choose between your addiction and finding a place— your life is too chaotic—you can't possibly take your medications on time, get a refill, go see your doctor. I mean all those things that we do—*Oh, I'll just put my next doctor's appointment on my iPhone calendar*—that's because we aren't living in complete chaos. It's the tip of the iceberg—but to ask someone who doesn't even know where they're going to sleep tonight to call the pharmacy before they run out of their medications, to even take their meds, won't work.

You try to help patients the best you can. But you're never going to solve addiction, or homelessness—or any of the social problems that make people fall through the cracks—you won't solve them at the ER during that one- or two-hour visit.

JOYCE AND EDDIE

He was a therapist, she was a nurse. But they met dancing. He brought her out of her shell, she encouraged him to take his writing seriously. They married, each their second, bought a home in the Santa Rosa hills, and brought their families together. In 2017, wildfires consumed the entire range, spilling over the nearest mountains and into the valley where they lived. That summer, the country had weathered a series natural disasters: flooding in Houston, hurricanes in Florida and Puerto Rico, wildfires in California. As the whole nation was consumed by the elements, this couple floated like pieces of hot ash. They have been squatting recently in the empty home of a friend. She lays out a plate of cookies that their dog, Sam, immediately attacks.

Joyce: At first, it was, *Oh, this is an adventure.* And then it was, *What do you mean we can't go home?* And then, you know, you lose your way. You really do lose your way. . . . Or, at least we did.

Eddie: I was in such denial to start with. We headed to stay with friends in Marin, and then family in Oakland. Along the way, we stopped at a Costco. We don't own anything anymore, so we started buying all these irrational things. We didn't have any underwear.

Joyce: "Where were you? What time did you leave?" Those were the two questions for weeks—still happens. We recognized each other, as survivors. We stopped at Kaiser, in Petaluma, to get some medications because all of our medications were gone. And you could just look at people and you could tell.

Eddie: Running into people looking for underwear. . . . They looked like zombies. We were nuts by then.

Joyce: You were nuts. I was numb.

She opens her computer and begins scrolling through photos: her garden, a bench embraced by flowers, light breaking through tree branches, then dark soil—no, not soil, ash—charred stone and leveled ground.

Joyce: We went up with family to go through and find things. We were going to look for my wedding ring. That was the big thing. And look for the lockbox that had our bonds in it and whatever else we could find. There was nothing to take away because it's all burned and charred and in pieces. The only thing left was a statue of the Buddha, sitting on the front lawn. My grandson, Devin, kept saying, "I think this would make a good art piece, Grandma." And I said, "Oh God. I don't think so. It's not my style."

Eddie: Eric, my son-in-law, said, "I think we found your dad!" I've had my dad and mom's ashes on the shelf because I didn't know what to do with them.

Joyce: That was the first bit of humor: "We're going to go up there and find those two brass boxes, going, 'Hello.'" But oh my God, every now and then I think about the things that are gone. Eddie lost all his poems, all his journals, all the anthologies that he was published in.

Eddie: I can't even grapple with it. It's like phantom pain. Like the limb is still there.

Joyce: The wall of kid paintings. Every one of the grandchildren is represented on there and they're all nicely framed and signed by these little scrawny kids. I loved that wall. I looked at that wall all the time. And even just a couple weeks before the fire, I thought . . . I don't know. We have three grandchildren getting married in the next year, year and a half. And I thought, *I'm going to reframe those and give it to them as wedding presents. Wouldn't that be fun?*

Eddie: The heart of the family is wherever we are—we know that. But for so long, that was the physical place of it. We were married in '91, and we bought in '92. We bought it a year after it was built. It was full of light, lots of windows.

Joyce: We ended up making a beautiful home. And, not in a hoity-toity way, but beautiful: our families blended there. Eddie's kids and eventually grandkids, and my kids and my grandkids. . . . And our parents were still alive. Everybody gathered at that house. Our grandchildren don't know anything else. The kids played baseball and rode their bikes down there because we were at the bottom of the circle. It was a safe place to be.

Eddie: Joyce has a huge heart. She is a natural nester.

Joyce: I had a conscious dream that just kept going for days and days and days. I saw the flames . . . I felt like they were just eating everything. And I walked through every room in my house and saw all the things that I love, not expensive stuff, and watched the flames come up.

Eddie: The dreams are interesting. I dreamed of a red bear.

Joyce: I remember sitting on my son's deck in Oakland one night. I had been doing pretty well. You know, tears but no real weeping. They had gone out, and Eddie was watching TV. And I went out on this beautiful deck just as the lights were coming on, on the bridges. And I was sitting there going, *This is such a beautiful sight . . . but I want to go home. I want my home. I want my imperfect life back. I don't want somebody else's life. I want mine.* I went inside and opened up a suitcase full of donated clothes. *I want my own clothes, but I don't have my own clothes except what I wore out of the fire.* My friends surprised me with these little Christmas ornament gifts. I couldn't even open them. *I don't want to be this person. I don't want to be the victim here. I don't want to be the survivor. I don't want this. I want to go back to what I*—[*She begins crying.*] I will not leave this community. I was born and raised here, most people aren't. I'm not going anywhere. I am blooming where I was planted.

Eddie: But you know what I find ironic about this? California's known for its environmental integrity. And still, we couldn't control this. That shows you the power—you can't plan for this anymore.

Joyce: No one is safe. I realize, for at least a month after the fire, I didn't wake up to other people's plight. I was so enveloped in trying to put one foot in front of the other. Listen to all the instructions from the police, from FEMA, from insurance, from my son, from the bank, from this, from that. Trying to keep things straight in my own mind, I carried these satchels around with all the papers of what we were trying to do. But I wasn't thinking about what other people were going through. And then I started thinking, *Houston, Puerto Rico, Florida. Times this by five thousand. How are people doing this? Are people as confused and strung out as we are? How are those people making it happen? How did they survive?* Until you've lived it, you don't get it. You really don't.

Eddie: We all live in tribes.

Joyce: Until you're standing in front of someone and listening to them with your own ears, you're never going to understand them.

ROB GITIN

He started an organization called At the Crossroads that walks the streets of the city each night bringing food, health and hygiene supplies, and counseling to homeless kids.

started volunteering at a drop-in center in San Jose. Every homeless kid downtown was coming to this place. I was nineteen, and the kids were roughly the same age as me. In a weird way, it was like the street being brought into this private setting. One that I was never privy to—condensed into this little space.

Kids were being real. I was struck by how raw everything was. How raw the humor was, how raw their stories were, even when they were brutal. In the moment, it didn't feel that emotional to hear because usually that's not the way kids were presenting it. It's not that they were breaking down weeping and telling you the story of the stepfather kicking them in the stomach when they came home and said, "I'm pregnant." He wanted to cause an abortion and succeeded, in this one girl's case.

They were telling you it as more kind of like, "Oh, here's a little background about me that gives context to the story that I'm telling now." And then you'd come home and think about how fucked up it was that they could normalize an experience like this.

The client who told me that story—I ended up learning half of what came out of her mouth was total BS. But you learn in this job you don't worry about the veracity of something; there's a reason they're communicating it. Even if the story is untrue, the feeling is usually real.

So I'd had this long conversation with her—and this was at a time where she wasn't really talking much to anyone else. And I figure I'm going to get a pat on the back, metaphorically, from Ernest and Jose, the two leaders of the place. Because she has opened up to me about shit that I knew she'd never opened to anyone else about.

And Ernest just looks at me and is like, "You fucked up today."

And I'm like, "What?"

"Rob, where is she going tonight?"

"I don't know."

"That's right, you don't know. She's going to sleep under a bridge. What is she doing before she goes to sleep?"

"I don't know."

"She's turning tricks. So do you think that it is a good thing that now she is thinking about the fact that her grandfather molested her while she's turning tricks at the hands of strange old men? Or do you think it's better that she kept that bottled up for tonight?"

The privilege that I'd come from, there was a cultural assumption that anytime you're dealing with something it's a good thing. That you have the physical and emotional safety net to catch you—so if thinking about those things rocks you a bit, it doesn't cause you harm. All I did is open a can of worms that, for her survival, was better off closed. *Okay, lesson learned.*

Our clients have been poked and prodded and analyzed and systematized and had so many things done to them against their will by people who were supposed to help them. They respond really well to just a person being there for them in whatever way they do or don't want that person to be there for them: Where that person isn't analyzing them, they're not delving deep into their past, they're not trying to take them places they don't want to go. They're just going with them wherever they want to go, being of support and helping them make sense of things.

You don't have to be a therapist to be able to do that. You have to have a certain makeup, and then you have to be trained well. But sometimes ways that people get trained as therapists can interfere with just listening.

It makes me think about a scene in *Bowling for Columbine*. Marilyn Manson was being interviewed, and the interviewer asked him if he could have talked to Dylan Klebold, and whoever the other kid was, what would he have said to them? And he said something like, "I wouldn't have said a thing. I would have listened. Because that's what no one did."

In particular, there's one subset of kids that have a really hard time accessing services: the kids who would tell you they'd known about the center for years before they ever set foot in it. Why aren't these kids coming in sooner? We learned that there are personal barriers that they face that make it hard to ask for help. It could be that they were beaten up or raped by a kid who goes to that place every day. But a lot of it has to do with losing hope, so why bother trying to get help?

And so we started going to different neighborhoods at different times of night, going up to any kids who looked even vaguely homeless, and saying, "Hey, we got some money to start doing this. What do you want to see?"

The kids were telling us overwhelmingly, "We want you to bring the services to us." And that's a reflection of survival culture. It's not about them being lazy, it's like, "My life is about hustling and surviving 24/7. If I have to take a bus for an hour and then sit somewhere and wait for an hour, I'm not going to do it."

So we had a couple of supplies on us and would go up to kids and offer them. In a way, it was utterly natural: "How are you doing? Do you need some socks tonight? Do you need a snack tonight?" But it often felt exhausting and completely inorganic. Like if you went to a party and you were tasked with the job of getting to know every single person by the end.

The number of times you get, "Get the fuck out of my face!" or "Who the fuck are you?" Or people threatening to hit you if you don't leave, that happens. As long as you understand where it's coming from, you don't sweat it, you don't take it personally.

Now it's different. Now we're out there and three-quarters of the kids we know and half of them are coming up and giving us a hug before we even see them. After having done this for seventeen years, those streets feel like home.

We've created this structure here where it's purely about the relationship. "You're smoking crack on the streets? Great, don't blow it in my face. You're about to get in a fight? Well, we'll walk away because we don't want to get in the middle of it, but we don't have to stop you from doing it. You're using racial epithets? Use them until you're blue in the face." And then our work in the daytime is one-to-one. So the time spent is just connecting with people.

As long as kids aren't hurting anyone or hurting themself, we support them in whatever life they want to build for themself. And it doesn't matter what that looks like. It doesn't matter to us if that involves school or work or housing. Now, the reality is that those are things most kids want. They want a legal income, so they want to work. They want stable housing, they want a home, they want healthy relationships. But we don't have to force them into it.

There was a kid, the first four years she wanted to work with us, she wanted me to buy her lunch and just receive her anger and profanity. She'd curse me out, she'd yell at me, she'd call me every name in the book, she'd rage against me. That's what she wanted, so that's what we gave. Eventually it gave way to her wanting to get off the streets, stop drinking a liter of vodka a day, stop doing two grams of heroin. So then we were able to help her with that. But you have to be willing to help with the first part for the kid to let you help with the second.

We do not save lives here, and we are really clear about that. You will never see in our literature or hear a counselor say, "Yeah, we save lives here." It's disrespectful, it's disempowering, and it can be patronizing. My brother-in-law saves lives, he's an emergency physician. We don't. We help them, we support them, we empower them, we bear witness, we assist. Choose your verb, but "save" is not among them.

Downtown has changed dramatically. When we first started working, maybe about 75 percent of the kids we saw were white, and then maybe a quarter black. The white kids, they ruled the night.

We'd sit down with a group of twenty crusty gutter-punk kids. They'd all be sitting in a circle or in little packs drinking, smoking weed, doing drugs, whatever. We'd kind of break up the circle a little and squeeze in between two kids to chat with them. A beer would pass by you; a joint would pass by you. They'd offer it, you'd say no. You'd offer them stuff, you'd chat with them, then you'd move one down and you'd move one down. We'd spend an hour or two just in that one circle of kids.

But then the neighborhood started to change. The white kids were getting targeted more by law enforcement. They were getting pushed to other neighborhoods, they were getting locked up, or services were reaching out to them. And so slowly, little by little we were seeing fewer and fewer white kids there.

Then there was the growth of the black community in youth street culture. It went from seeing five black kids a night to ten to fifteen to twenty. To now, on a typical night we might see fifty black kids and five kids from other ethnic backgrounds.

The black kids don't look stereotypically homeless, so no homeless services are targeting them. It's why their needs are getting so underserved. At the beginning, we did not know what the hell we were doing with the black kids out there. We'd be like, *Are they homeless? Are they not? Should we be targeting them? Should we not?*

It's funny, you learn to notice differences. You see that the same kid has been wearing the same outfit for four straight days. Or they don't smell great and they probably haven't showered in a couple days. Or all their stuff, while it looks clean, it's not name-brand. And when we really clarified the term "underserved homeless youth," it was like a light went on: *Holy shit. The black kids are exactly who we need to reach.* Because no one was prioritizing them.

And over time, that resolve has grown even stronger. A, these kids aren't being identified by the city, by service providers, by anyone—and, B, most of them do not identify as homeless.

When people in San Francisco think of homeless youth, they think of dirty white kids. Kids who actively reject the system, who project themselves as anarchists, "Man, the system fucked me, so fuck the system."

And black kids are like, "No, no, I am not a Haight Street kid!" Very, very clearly that is not who they are. And so because of that they're not going to go and seek out homelessness services, they're not going to go into a drop-in center, they're not going to go into a job program for homeless people.

Then there's another issue. The black kids that we work with have grown up in lots of different houses with cousins, with aunts, with uncles. That's not shaming or labeling. That's part of the reality of being poor and black in this city, in this country. It's part of being targeted by law enforcement, being incarcerated, and having your family broken up time and time again.

As the black population in San Francisco has shrunk, we've seen a rise in the number of black homeless youth. And we've tried to make sense of it. Thirty-five years ago, when San Francisco was 14 percent black, a sixteen-year-old black kid—if their pseudo-nuclear home wasn't working out—they had options. They had five, ten, fifteen different relatives, different households that provided opportunities other than a street. Well, now all those relatives have moved away.

So now rather than having a few different places that they can stay for six months here, three months there, two months there—or even a night here, a night there—those places don't exist anymore. Those places are now in Antioch, they're in Sacramento, they're in Vallejo. Or they've just left the Bay Area completely.

Many white kids wear their homelessness like a badge of courage: "Being homeless was the safest and smartest option for me. So why would I be embarrassed about that?" There's no condemnation of people that they *love*. There might be condemnation of people they *hate* in saying, "I'm homeless."

For the black kids, so much of their support comes from friends and family, churches, the community. They take the place of social services, which often fail these kids. I've always wondered if part of the reason that so many black youth don't identify as homeless is out of a fear that it implies that their community of friends and family also failed them.

Black kids don't sleep on the streets, almost never. They will find any other alternative. They want to be able to keep a certain appearance. It's why a white kid is more comfortable panhandling—make enough money to support your drug habit and your food. Whereas the black kids are more focused on making money out there because they're trying to pay for a hotel room every night so that they're not sleeping on the streets. They often don't think of themselves as homeless.

But if you ask them the question, "When is the last time you had a stable place to stay?" they'd be like, "I don't know. Five years ago, eight years ago, twelve years ago."

SAMMY NUNEZ

He felt lost—he had seen his family worn to shreds working the fields of California's farms, watched his father and brothers drift in and out of prison, his community torn apart by drugs, prostitution, poverty. He could still feel the shotgun wound in his shoulder healing, years later. He turned to indigenous medicine, sweat ceremonies: "Since time immemorial, we've had methods of healing, creating equilibrium and balance. How do you raise Chicano men of color, boys of color, to be brave, to be truthful, you know, to be compassionate? I felt something stirring within my spirit, a kind of jump, wakening a feeling like I had been here before." The organization he started, Fathers and Families of San Joaquin, has broad reach into the city of Stockton. They act almost as a parallel government, serving those forgotten by a once-forgotten city. Stockton is over two hours from the Bay Area and has slowly felt the ripples of change radiating from San Francisco and Silicon Valley. Recently, those ripples have grown to waves as those displaced from the Bay Area have started to crash on Stockton's shores.

For many, this is the place of last resort. There's a mass influx, an exodus. Poor people are getting pushed out of the Bay, pushed right to our community. It's forced migration.

They arrive totally dislocated. Rattled, shell-shocked. Stockton is not Oakland. The weather's different. The way things flow is different. We have our own *get down* out here.

And we don't have the resources to actually support these folks. We don't have the same infrastructure, the same opportunities, the same culture. There's a disparity, a regional disparity in terms of the reinvestment and resources. The Bay has a plethora of social justice–type organizations there. Here, there's very few. This is traditionally a conservative stronghold. People proudly say, "We're not the Bay," you know.

It's kind of a cruel irony. The Central Valley is an agricultural hub, if you will. We feed the world, yet we have some of the worst food insecurity here. Private industry and developers pretty much control the politics in Stockton—they got rich. So you've got tremendous wealth with punctuated poverty. Some of the deepest racism and segregation. Our school system is failing our children: third-highest illiteracy rate in the nation, the highest in the state, you have some schools with zero percent literacy. Double the national average for unemployment, so there's not a lot of opportunity for upward mobility. Slumlords, squalor, horrid living conditions. We have some of the worst air quality here. Crazy corrupt government. Indictments for embezzlement. Our politicians not in the headlines for the right reasons.

These are global issues, and they're concentrated in Stockton. This was ground zero for the housing crisis. One of the largest metropolitan cities to file for bankruptcy. California is, what, the fifth- or sixth-largest economy in the world? And we have poverty comparable to third-world conditions? It's criminal. You have this storm—perfect storm—of poverty, despair, and oppression.

Now you add to that these folks that are being gentrified from the Bay Area.

They put pressure on the community, on the grassroots, on the underground economy. It has created a real flash point, a lot of tension. Violence across the United States has dropped; violence in Stockton is on the uptick. Folks are bringing their neighborhoods, their banners, their flags into Stockton. Whole gangs from Oakland are moving into this area and are obviously having conflict with the indigenous organizations. We get a lot of folks from Oakland coming to Stockton to bury their relatives. I would call it a crisis.

We have to create a paradigm shift. If they aren't actively

involved and engaged in the process, that means we have to engage them.

So every day, when somebody from Oakland comes into our offices—or we get a call from sister agencies in Oakland telling us some of their folks are here now and are homeless, or they're in crisis, or somebody got shot—we respond. Because, the way I see it, they're not Oaklanders. They live in our city. Now they're *Stocktonians*.

We're sort of the brokers, I guess you can say, to what other folks consider "hard-to-reach communities." I was at a presentation, all these organizations talking about "hard-to-reach communities." And I was like, "No. *We're* not hard to reach. *Y'all* are hard to reach. We don't find you in our neighborhoods. We have access to probation officers, and that's pretty much it." Victims of violence become violent. Parents teach their kids how to survive incarceration. When you're unemployed, you're hungry, you're basically homeless—and you got a gun—something bad is gonna happen.

Now if crime harms, justice should heal. We just need the political will to create this collective healing.

So we are the rising tide that lifts all ships. Whether that's shrinking the prison population or improving reentry. Whether that's climate change and climate investment here locally. Childhood, parenthood, neighborhood. Strong families create strong communities.

We've been at it for twenty years, building this movement on the ground. We have call-in lines for legal questions, questions about public services. We host an elder circle every day. We intervene in domestic violence incidents. We beautify the parks and provide after-school programs for kids. We are doing everything the government can't. We're the most transformative, the most engaged, the most responsive organization on the ground out here, and we can barely keep up.

Resiliency, hope, heart. Look, if you're in Stockton, man, you've gotta have heart and you've gotta have a thick skin. You gotta have grit, you know what I'm saying, if you're gonna survive in this city.

Whether you were born here or you've come here, we're rewriting our future together. And Stockton is starting to emerge and become a kind of breakthrough community. We'll even teach the Bay a thing or two.

TITUS BELL (CONT'D)

We meet in the Outer Mission, by the Muni tracks where he was arrested for armed robbery when he was sixteen. He was released from prison three years ago and has stayed out of trouble since.

My closest friend, he's locked up right now for murder. It was about three years ago, on Valentine's Day.

My birthday is the day before. He called me, wished me a happy birthday. I was *this close* to kicking with them that night too. But I was with my girl, and I was like, "I'm kinda tired. Let's just go home."

He rode out and shot at some people down on Fifteenth. Got in a high-speed, and it was over after that. The cops started chasing him, and he crashed into one car, took out the passenger. And that car crashed into some dude that was walking to the store.

The next morning, it was like, "Dude, where's Goldie?" It was like, "We can't find him. He's not at home." Because he would always say, "Oh, I'm home and safe" at the end of the night, and he didn't do that.

And then my homie who lives down in Fremont was like, "Brah, turn on the news." And it was everywhere. I'm like, "Damn! That's crazy! Like I was just talking to the man last night!" And I coulda been there too.

That goes to show, girls will keep you safe! I'm telling you. Listen to your girl; she'll keep you safe.

I had to reevaluate myself. Had I stayed in the streets, things were getting pretty serious. It wasn't fun and games anymore. That *reputation*, that *wanting power*. We were getting to the point where it was getting super dangerous, and we felt like we didn't have no other choice.

So I started kicking with different people.

I started hanging out with my girl more. And she showed me, like, "Oh, you go to a job. You go to work." I had never seen that before. I had never been around people who actually go to work every day to pay rent. She worked at Chipotle and this little sushi spot. I was twenty years old and still in high school. I'm like, *Okay, let me get this done.* After I was done with high school, I was able to work more. I was able to earn a little bit more money, so it made sense to me. Like, *Oh, more education, more money. . . .*

Now I'm at City College. This is my last semester. It's just so much information. I feel like my brain is about to implode.

Most people who go through what I go through have so much hate in their heart, so much anger. They see the gloom and the dark side—they can't see things like this. I have a weird sense of humor, and people like being around that. I love that feeling. That same feeling that I was getting in the streets, I was getting in those jobs and stuff.

I don't want to be sixty-five, here, in a small apartment in the Tenderloin. So what do I need to do? Oh, I'm gonna go to law school. Dang, I want to go to Harvard! I can taste it! I saw the Obama movie and it made so much sense to me. It takes a high, high, high, high, *high* assimilation to get into places of power. But then the powers have to start listening to you. I want to open up my own law firm—a nonprofit law firm—educate people.

It's the most simple thing. To take genuine interest into someone's life: *Your life, your human life, you are a precious human being. And I love everything about you.* That mind frame: companionship is essential!

And once you surround yourself with those people, then you get what you deserve. I mean, you get what you want.

PART V

IF WE CAN
MERGE THE
TWO WORLDS

"Tech" is not a monolith, the public sector is not a single body, and those who fight for social justice do not speak in a common voice. As tempting as it may be to describe San Francisco as a tale of two cities, there is no single fault line that describes how the city is being divided.

The Bay Area has weathered the social and economic equivalent of a great earthquake: A shock, born of friction building beneath our feet, that shakes everyone's foundations but leaves the most vulnerable structures broken. There are cracks in the pavement everywhere. Important issues are pulling public attention in so many directions that none get the support they need. And, just as San Francisco did after the earthquakes in 1906 and 1989, it will have to build again.

It will take time to heal, to rebuild infrastructure and institutions, common ground and communal will. It will take time and *presence*, the ability to wait, to listen, to learn from others, and to see the important nuances. The smallest cracks are easy to overlook and will only grow larger.

Happily, the region has many healers, folks who picked a rift in the ground and are patiently coaxing it to close: activists push large companies to create a more diverse workplace, labor movements forge unexpected alliances to fight for fairer wages, engineers partner with government to defend the environment, and leaders try to build bridges (sometimes literally) to knit the community back together.

NICOLE SANCHEZ

Growing up, she had a keen sense for injustice. "My mom always told me I've been wired this way. I think probably a lot of people who identify as activists are wired this way." Even in college, she saw the chasm widening between the tech and wider communities. She now works as a diversity consultant for the tech industry.

n tech, there is a derogatory term for somebody like me, do you know what it is? "Social Justice Warrior." "SJW" is how you'll see it.

Someone once said, "Doesn't that sound awesome? 'Social Justice Warrior'? Wouldn't you be so happy to be called that?" And I was like, "Yeah, you would think so in a vacuum. But it's the shorthand for 'these lefty assholes.'"

If you go on Twitter and search for "SJW," the kind of things you will see are horrific. About those of us who are trying to bring social justice into the fold of technology. Which I absolutely am unabashedly trying to do. I'm not even going to pretend like I'm not.

This is an epochal battle. So much of tech is driven by people who believe in a libertarian change model—they like to pretend they are just building tools and are neutral politically. You can't be neutral. If you have no orientation—*whatever happens, happens*—that's a bias.

I was at Stanford from 1990 to 1994. It was a really hard time to decide that racial and social justice was going to be the thing that you cared about. We had affirmative action backlash. Prop 187 passed right after I graduated—an anti-immigration bill that targeted Mexicans in particular.* And then Prop 209 shortly after that, which gutted affirmative action in public schools.† Condoleezza Rice was our provost. And so, this was the climate. I was miserable.

Tons of the people who espoused this libertarian model were there at the same time. They did *not* have neutral opinions about politics then, and I don't believe that they had some sort of transformational experience later on that reshaped their sense of justice. I don't. I can tell you stories about them; they would tell you stories about me; and both our stories would be pretty much in line with what we're all doing now.

And so it's continued to be the same fight in a different arena—then and now. An age-old struggle. A lifelong battle with a very similar cast of characters. So when people say, "But

---

* Proposition 187 prohibited illegal aliens from using state resources, in particular the public universities and schools that had become an important part of California's identity. Though federal and state courts blunted the measure, it stayed on the books for twenty years until the state legislature finally repealed the unconstitutional elements of the law.

† Though Proposition 209 has been the subject of several legal challenges and persistent protest, the law remains in effect as of publication.

haven't you heard the latest from"—fill in the blank. I'm like, "That dude? That dude carved 'fag' into the door of one of my friends' rooms when we were eighteen years old. Let me tell you how much I trust *that* person." Most of my people have left tech or never joined in the first place because they're like, "I don't want to be around those people."

These are people who have no humanities background, so they have no fluency in the language of social justice. There is a person who is very well known in Silicon Valley, who has funded many, many, many companies, who will regularly go on rants on Twitter about how humanities majors are wrecking technology. I want to tell them, they just need a little exposure—read *A People's History of the United States*, listen to a speech by Shirley Chisholm. You'll realize, *Oh, I can re-imagine everything!*

One of the things that makes me effective today is that I can see this stuff coming from a mile away. We were one of the only Mexican families where I grew up. My sisters and I very much got told, "You have to be twice as good. You have to be twice as fast." All that stuff. But my dad, being a mathematician, would tell us, "Look. The story goes you have to be twice as good to be seen as half as worthy, which means you have to be four times . . ." Ha-ha-ha! No pressure at all!

When I got accepted into Stanford, people said, "Well, we know how you got in. . . ." The same people who had been praising me, who had voted for me for student body president, who had come to cheer me on when we won the softball championship—the same people could pull the rug out from under you. I had a teacher—her "fave" didn't get into Stanford for whatever reason—she gave us this whole speech about how mediocrity rises to the top and then said, "*You* know what I mean, Nicole?"

I don't have to have it decoded for me anymore. I go, "No, I totally understand what you're saying. Please, stop talking, because I absolutely understand." Even the person perpetrating it sometimes doesn't understand how it is unfolding into a very racist rant. And you go, "Hold up. I think you're gonna want to stop right there. Let me explain to you where this is going." And it's shocking to white folks.

My first job in diversity-and-tech was 1999. We've been ignored; we've been laughed at; now we're in the fight—absolutely in fighting mode. And the shift that comes is that things start to get a little more nuanced.

The mental gymnastics are more complicated. It's less about educating and more about what we really do with that awareness. So the conversation stops being "Diversity isn't important." The conversation is "Great. You know you sound outdated if you say that diversity isn't important. But the interventions that you put in place are often wrong. They're just wrong."

I've worked hard to professionalize diversity work. There are so many companies that will say, "Oh, I'm just going to call that black woman engineer and see what she thinks about diversity, because she must know the answer . . ." What the hell? She's spent her training learning how to be an engineer. She's got a lot of lived experience, which is great, but diversity work is not her field. Her deal is engineering. Please give her the room to be a successful engineer and hire people who do this thing for a *living*.

You wouldn't have a non-accountant counting your money. You wouldn't go to someone with no background in cloud computing and say, "What do you think we should do about migrating everything to the cloud?" Right? Simultaneously, if this is not your discipline—and I'm not just saying, "Are you a person of color? Are you a woman?"—if this is not your *discipline*, you can be *helpful*, but you cannot *lead* this conversation.

Because we will tell you, you cannot program your way out of this problem. There is no algorithm that will solve this. Bias continues to be embedded in the code.

Many of the solutions that will bring about racial-social justice, put an end to police violence, do those kinds of things—need to have, at their root, technology.

Technology, to scale. Technology, for accessibility. Technology, for low-cost solutions and low barriers to entry. Technology in and of itself is going to be a critical part of the movement. Twitter itself has been a critical part of bringing Black Lives Matter to the forefront. That was in spite of what Twitter thought it was doing!

This is the place where stuff is scalable, where we will start to build apps that are about access to clean water and not delivering food to my doorstep. This is the moment when we can merge the amazingness of Silicon Valley technology and the Bay Area's roots in protest politics and social justice.

If we can merge the two worlds, we stand a chance.

CHARLES CARTER (CONT'D)

Sitting on his porch, he fell silent. He had finished describing his career, then nodded and leaned forward—I thought, as if to get up, extend his hand, and conclude the interview. Instead, he rested his elbows on his knees and stared out across the street where a neighbor was mending part of his roof.

'*ve always struggled to reconcile the benefits of California with the* ambition you need to reap those benefits. I'm still struggling with that.

Europeans came to California out of ambition, quickly recognized how special the place is. The human duality—we're part of nature, yet we need to control it, subdue it. So at the same time we discovered the environmental benefits of this place, we learned it had raw materials to support other endeavors. Across the history of the state, you see these instincts in tension—environmentalism and development, restraint and greed.

I'm part of that story. Growing up in Pennsylvania, my dad told me the Jackie Robinson story, about how he went to UCLA and did all these wonderful things. I was a big Brooklyn Dodger fan, and when the Dodgers moved, I said, "I'm gonna go to California." The Gold Rush never ended, right? Everybody was gonna go to California, and do whatever they couldn't do wherever they were.

I'm a trained physical designer, I'm a landscape architect. Most of us think we're gonna go be protectors of the environment. I like to make pretty things. I like to know the names of the trees and the birds around me. I came here in an interesting time, the '70s and '80s, when people were looking for ways to harmonize growth with these more noble, if you will, objectives to protect this wildly fantastic environment.

So I'm all about *place*. Humans get fixated on their social place and have lost touch with the physicality of it. As much as we're masters of our planet, and can go anywhere and do anything at any time, our spaces still define the boundaries of our behavior. We get clues on how to be, from our environment. The more disconnected you are from it, the more lost you are, as how to be as a species, an organism, an individual.

The challenge is, how do we build great societies without great machines that deplete the resources that enable it in the first place? We need to understand how it all fits together better, not that any one way is right or wrong. We were local creatures once, and we will remain local creatures for a long time to come. Maybe we have to revisit the model of everybody having a means to get anywhere within five hundred miles in a single day.

The original purpose of technology was to provide greater

material comfort for humans. With greater material comfort, we had more time for intellectual, cultural pursuits. It feels like, again, we've reached a point of diminishing returns. Man is the most successful organism that's walked this planet. How much better can we make it for him? How much more do we need?

Maybe because it happened in my lifetime, I've just been really skeptical about the information age and the benefits it's gonna reap. I don't know that it necessarily addresses what we struggle with as individuals or as communities.

Can we have broad-based, inclusive communities that are still economically vibrant? Can we avoid building what we, in the landscape business, call monocultures? Can we avoid narrowing the range of diversity of experience? Can we expand the access to opportunity? It doesn't look like technology has answers to these questions.

There's a physicality to our culture, a presence, that I think is being lost through technological manipulation. We may get to a point where the physical geographical associations aren't necessary anymore, because we connect other ways, but is there a point we become too disembodied?

I don't know that what California is producing now, as a sustainable crop, can sustain a population or a growth in population for a long time.

COCO CONN (CONT'D)

In the '80s and '90s, inspired by the expansive spirit of early innovators, she started teaching and leading expos, bringing technology to children around the world. Her approach was inspired by her daughter: "When she was two years old, she was on a Macintosh already, using MacPaint, and I thought, *Wow, this is great.* At first, I thought she was unique, someone so young adapting to this technology, until I realized this is the only technology she had ever used. Of course she was going to adapt to it. The people that hadn't grown up with it, they were the ones that were struggling to learn it at all."

A friend of mine wanted kids to build a city on the internet. This was '93. There wasn't even an internet then, but he wanted kids to collaborate. I brought in some high-end engineers. We got access to some military software. We took the *aim*, *shoot*, and *kill* functionality out of it. And so, we had a place for the kids to build.

We did a little traveling road show. We held tutorials at museums and science centers, teaching kids how to model. And whatever they would create would go in the city. We weren't really *teaching*. We were just asking the kids to build a city.

There were very few boundaries because schools were terrified of technology because, to them, that meant money and budgets. They couldn't afford it. So I would come in behind the scenes . . . I would bring in the administrators and the teachers and say, "Look, we're not teaching anything. The kids teach themselves."

We'd say, "Here's how to make a box, how you extrude the box. Here's how you make a window." The basics of computer graphics, the building blocks are so simple. And with that little bit of information, they'd say, "Okay, now I'm gonna put some instruments in the wall and I need a chair." And it was wild: by leaps and bounds they were building this massive city.

We were just kludging. But it was amazing how advanced we were. All my friends were coming in saying, "We were talking

about building this technology, and you guys are here *doing* it."
We were doing VR before there was VR.

You could see the city on the screen. We'd say to the kids,
"While you're building it, you can fly through the city." We
were connected over T1 lines—which was unusual at the
time—so they were flying through the model in real time. We
built a controller box so you could jump to different parts, like
teleporting.

It was really beautiful. It was very expansive. It had a dark
background. Tall buildings. One kid built a very, very tall building, and the other kids were up in arms. They all had a meeting
about how tall the building could be. One little girl was making
furniture, beautiful furniture. And one of the boys put her furniture in his casino, and oh my God, she was so upset.

She said, "You can't use my furniture for that."

And he said, "Okay, let's find a way to make this work. How
about I donate all the proceeds from my casino?"

And she said, "Oh, that's a great idea."

Technology can awaken children. The most critical thing is
that you reach people while they still have their self-esteem and
a willingness to learn. If we don't use this technology in clever
ways for the younger generation, we're missing the real reason to
have these things in the classroom. It's not just about entertain-
ing and engaging. It's how do these technologies help us evolve
to the next step in our evolution—in a way that helps the planet.

I've been watching cuttlefish on the internet. They have only
a two-year life-span. They die shortly after they mate. But most
amazing, they have this ray-tracing machine inside them—their
little brains can control these pixels on their body. I think there's
four colors on each pixel, and so you're watching this animal
and, depending on its situation, it can completely animate itself.
It's so brilliant!

I'm fascinated by this instinct to adapt.

Some of my philosophy friends say there's people that believe, ultimately, we need to get off this planet. Because we're destroying it and it's only gonna last so long anyways. So no matter how long we're on the planet, there's gonna be this fixation to get off of it.

We can't send humans into space, because they'll die. We don't have years to travel to the next galaxy. So maybe on some weird level, we are destined to create a cyborg version of ourselves that can travel. Maybe some of the technology today is helpful to the survival of the species thousands of years from now, even millions of years from now. We don't know what's driving it. We don't know if we've been here before.

But we are going to adapt. We're hardwired to do it, like the little cuttlefish. If we have three eyes, then fine, we'll have three eyes. We are ruining the planet, so it doesn't matter, in the long run, whether we destroy our bodies or ourselves. We're all going to mutate together.

SAUL GRIFFITH (CONT'D)

Whether it was trying to build more efficient carburetors for the family car, or novel printing presses for his mother, he had always been inventive. He got accepted into MIT "through the tradesman's entrance" and exited with a PhD. He graduated determined to defend the environment and moved to San Francisco because it had the best windsurfing. It also had a culture that embraced his instincts: "There's a narrative that exists here, an ecosystem where you can do some of these things. I just worry it's batting above its real contribution."

did metallurgical engineering for my undergraduate engineering degree. One and a half years of which I was working in industry. I worked at a steel research facility. I worked at a blast furnace. I worked at a steel-rolling mill. I worked at an aluminum smelter. I saw three men die in that period.

One guy got caught between a train coupling that was bringing in the raw materials. One guy got hit by a piece of rebar that was at 1200 degrees Celsius. And the other one was probably a suicide underneath a hydraulic industrial lift. I saw the pool of blood and I reported it in at maintenance as "The hydraulic fluid is leaking in the elevator." Then I realized, as we walked back, *Oh shit. It's blood.*

These are just brutal industries. Australia still, including culturally, is roughly California of 1880 or 1890. We do two things. We do tourism. And then we do coal, and iron ore, and bauxite, and uranium. So Australia is a prehistoric economy based on raping the land and selling the friendliness of your people to the highest bidder.

I grew up in an environment where we cared greatly about the natural world. My mother painted Australia's natural landscape. For six weeks each year, we would go to some World Heritage Area or some national park. We would go to these amazing places. I would carry the camera gear and take photographs for my mother that she would use as reference material to paint.

I have tried to spend my whole working life trying to unfuck the planet. We're on a horrible trajectory. But how do you make the biggest difference? What actually can work at a scale to solve the problem? The biggest of those problems is climate change.

I could employ myself and twenty thousand other people on the problems to solve climate change for the rest of my life. And we try to work on the most impactful things, giant economic opportunities. We don't all want to live in caves, so how do you build the compromise between what culture and society want to be and what is physically possible?

I wish I could paint you a narrative: *There is an easy pathway to a beautiful world. We have more great technology than ever before to do more great things. Everything works. We all work less. We live amongst gardens. There is every reason to hope.* But I am a little dark these days.

It used to be different. Prior to the 1990s, venture capital actually did difficult things, like funding companies like Intel. And there was a history of doing super-ambitious, hard, high-capital things. But everyone got drunk and giddy building companies like Google, which were low capital, high profits.

You *should* be able to go to a venture capitalist and say, "I'm really smart. Here's the math. You can check my homework. This will work." That doesn't get funded. No matter how much you hope it does.

Venture now funds you to expand your sales team. It doesn't fund you to do anything that's revolutionary anymore. Everyone wants to fund the Ubers and the Airbnbs, which really are not at all technological. They are leveraging government investments in technology to do economic and social disruption.

That will all be lost in the narrative of history, because Silicon Valley wants to have this libertarian idea that the government doesn't know how to spend money to do research, which couldn't be more contrary to the evidence. Search was first funded by DARPA. The internet was built by DARPA. GPS, accelerometers, they were funded by DARPA. Government funding did everything here, all the instruction, the training. The self-driving cars were a DARPA program twenty years ago. It wasn't invented by Sebastian Thrun, who will be now known as the inventor of the autonomous car. He won the *second* DARPA Grand Challenge, not the *first* one. He didn't even enter into the first one.

What enables Uber? The internet. GPS in every car, on every phone. A huge number of programming languages—the first thirteen layers of the software stack, all of that structure was written on government funds. They are driving on public roads. Half the innovations in cars were funded indirectly. So they are unbelievably subsidized.

Obama said at some speech—he phrased it very well—"You didn't build that." He was right, but it backfired. He got reamed. Still, it was astute and true. We give the government far too little credit for what it does. If you want to do anything interesting and important, by my definition, you pretty much end up at the government trough.

But then a whole bunch of libertarians want to think that it's their genius. No. What they've done is a really clever socioeconomic hack. In fact, it's not even that clever. It's cynical. They are exploiting loopholes and taking infrastructure for granted.

These are robber barons in the traditional sense.

Because it's this weird, extractive industry of eyeballs and attention. I do think Google tries to "do no evil" and all the rest, but merely trying not to do evil is not enough. So far they've really failed at doing anything except advertising. The organization has a personality, and, unfortunately, somehow the personality of that organism got away from them. I know very few assholes who work at Google. But the collective Google . . . is an asshole.

Google now spends about $9 billion on things that they call "research," which is larger than the National Science Foundation and DARPA's budget combined. And I would have to say it's the most inefficient and poorly spent money in the history of research in the United States. They are not rigorous and they don't listen to the external world. And their arrogance is profound.

Do the five companies currently supporting this bubble make anything that you would call a "staple"? They don't make staples of food. They don't make housing. They don't make transportation. They don't make water. They don't make energy. So it's kind of concerning. There was more sense to the world when Ford and GE were at the top of the US stock market.

Historically, at Otherlab, roughly half or more of our income has come from development research grants. And people at DARPA or ARPA-E have said to us, "You're our best performer ever. You're the only people who we give money to who do what they say they're going to do."[*] Because we do the analysis up front. We're not trying to maximize the amount of government money we get. We're trying to get the job done.

Sunfolding, natural gas, robotics, exoskeletons. We survived by becoming extremely good. I am capable of winning any junkyard-dog competition. I'll build you a satellite out of parts. But we are also more rigorous than the great majority of academics at the world's best universities. We could go toe-to-toe with any of them on physics and math.

This place is the union of rigor and fucking *make-it-work*. We have to be.

RON CONWAY (CONT'D)

Ed Lee was mayor of San Francisco for almost seven years, watching San Francisco transform during his two terms. He is widely criticized by many for accelerating the change, offering tax breaks to keep tech companies and their tax revenues in the city, but as a consequence injecting gentrification with a shot of adrenaline. He tried to find answers as the problems worsened—the housing crisis,

---

[*] Modeled after DARPA, the Advanced Research Projects Agency–Energy invests in the creation of advanced energy technologies.

rising homelessness, declining schools—but his tenure ended suddenly. On December 12, 2017, he died of a heart attack. In the weeks following, San Francisco began its search for another interim mayor.

'*ve been involved in San Francisco politics for about fifteen years, ever* since we moved back to the city. I got very active in the years Gavin Newsom was mayor. And then, when he was elected lieutenant of California, they were looking for a caretaker, kind of like the controversy that is going on now. They reached into the bowels of the city bureaucracy and found Ed Lee. He was running a big piece of the city bureaucracy. But I had never met him or even heard his name.

When he was appointed, we were in the 2008 recession, and San Francisco had 10 percent unemployment. Ed had a commonsense approach: *10 percent unemployment, this is a disaster! I'm just going to go work on getting that number down. And if I fix unemployment, that will fix a lot of the other problems in the city.*

So he called a meeting of tech leaders to come to City Hall. I was there. And he said, "What can I do to help you guys create more jobs in San Francisco?" We went through a litany of options, and he left with something like ten action items. Way too many!

I said, "With the approval of the other CEOs, I want you to leave with just two. Number one, we can't let Twitter move out of the city. They're already tech's second-biggest employer behind Salesforce." San Francisco was charging everyone payroll tax—whether you had revenue or not—and Twitter had revolted and threatened to move their headquarters. So what I said was, "You've got to create a payroll tax–free zone."

And number two, Yelp and Zynga were about to leave, because the city charged its own stock-option tax. Only city in the country to do that. Meaning no tech company would ever go public in San Francisco. Companies would move out of the city so that they wouldn't cost their employees the stock-option tax.

Ed Lee fixed those two issues in two months. He went to work. And I said, "Wow. This guy is something else."

Now ultimately, we fixed it for everybody. We passed Prop E a few years later, which changed the payroll tax for every company in the city to be a revenue-based tax, so that start-ups would not have this onerous payroll tax.

I told Ed he better run for mayor: "You're the best thing that ever happened to the city."

And he said, "No, no, no. I can't do that. I agreed to be just a caretaker." He was just as humble and soft-spoken as you can imagine.

The Chinese community was drafting him as well. Rose Pak launched the "Run, Ed Lee, Run" program all over the city. The Chinese community saying, "Hey, you're the first Chinese-American mayor. You're doing a good job, and we want to keep you!" That was what really got him to run.

His campaign motto was "Get Things Done."

And that's all he did, he just got things done. He was a bureaucrat that knew how to wiggle through the system and accomplish things to help the city. That's all he did twenty-four hours a day: find problems and go and solve them. He would know if somebody was bullshitting him, because he had done almost every job in the city!

He was a huge believer and promoter of public-private partnerships and would encourage those everywhere he possibly could.

Through the Navigation Centers, the city is slowly solving the homeless issue. They help people get off the street—no questions asked—bring all your stuff, bring your pet, bring a companion. Trying to get the edge cases, those hardest hit. Funny enough, the very first Navigation Center was funded by an anonymous tech donation of millions of dollars to test out the concept. There's four now, and the plan is to keep building more.

On housing, he wanted to build thirty thousand housing units by 2020 and that's going to happen.

The middle school program—he had a theory that kids get molded in middle school. He got Salesforce to donate $30 million—they adopted the schools—and now the program has expanded to Oakland. Ed Lee always said, "This is my legacy."

He was frustrated by the criticism, but every year the unemployment rate went down, tax revenue went way up, and he was able to put together the city programs that he always dreamed about. And he had the money to do it, because he had full employment. And the progressives who don't get that, they are never going to get it. But yes, that was a constant frustration.

Ed Lee's whole mantra was, *I'm just going to go do my job. I'm going to build more affordable housing. I'm going to go do what I know is right. Let them say what they want.*

And you know, actions speak louder than words.

NAVIDA BUTLER

The 101 highway runs down the east side of the San Francisco peninsula and divides Palo Alto from East Palo Alto. On one side, Stanford University and all it radiates. On the other, a small working-class town, once the per-capita murder capital of the US. Nearly one-fifth of East Palo Alto lives below the poverty line. Navida has run the Ecumenical Hunger Project since it was just a few drawers in her desk at the Red Cross. It has since grown into one of the largest aid organizations serving East Palo Alto's poor. She sits outside a warehouse of donated clothes and furniture, so she can personally welcome everyone who drops in.

was a runaway mom with three kids. I was homeless when I came here. I had no furniture. I stayed with people, with friends. In a friend's apartment, we slept on the floor. There were mice running everywhere. Two hours, I caught fourteen mice that got in the house. I set up traps—I'm from the South—they were popping everywhere.

I always wanted to come to California. You always think of gold when you think of California. And I was surprised by the poverty level here. Coming from the South and growing up in the country, there was always something to eat. You could always go get your wild animals, which Californians are so against. Here, you see a lot of poverty.

But I always will remember how I was treated by people. There was a lady over at the American Red Cross, Ruth Miles, took me under her wing. She gave me a job, trained me how to work with families. She used to tell me, "You can run this center over at the Red Cross." And I thought, *This lady has got to be crazy. I'm the only black that works here and the last to be hired, and I'm going to run this?* Before I left, I was the service center coordinator—over people that was there when I started.

That's part of why people come to California. I didn't believe it then, but people will tell you all the time—the laws and things about employment in California are special. Texas is a good example—you look at people the wrong way and they can fire you, let you go at will. In California, rights are more protected than back in the South.

The ability to make something out of your life, here, it's greater than any other place that I know. You're accepted. I don't think the color of your skin makes as much difference in California as it does in some of the other places. I really don't. I love the diversity here.

But there's a real breakdown. People are homeless. People are dying out there. And we need to see what we can do to help. I always felt, *if you don't care about people, this is not the place for you to work. Go on and work in a factory, work for a computer company. Here, you have lives. It has to touch your heart.*

A lot of people call me Momma. I do a lot of listening and talking to people. Sometimes, they need bus fare. Lack of food. Formula is very expensive. Somebody needs something special and the word goes out, like a ripple in the water. Soon, we'll just have to figure out how to get it from the donor to the person in need.

I'll always remember this young guy, he had cancer. Somebody told him if anybody could help, I could help. This guy was in his forties and my heart just went out to him. Too young. I shared his story with our board and, don't you know, they took up to help pay his rent.

Then, his landlord told him he was going to raise the rent because he was getting all of this help. Boy, did we chew that landlord out. He said, "Well, he was supposed to have been dead a long time ago."

"Oh my God, you didn't just say what I heard you say!" We shamed him into letting him stay there until he died. Each member of that board would go to the health-food store and buy some of the things that he needed.

I fuss at people. Even the young people. Sometimes, if they see me coming, they're going to hide. They know I'm going to say, "Why are you out here? This is not the place to be!"

I had this guy on my fence one day getting some fruit down off the tree. He's standing up on top of my fence, and I went out there and told him, "Get your behind off of that fence!"

My grandson is like, "Grandma, he's a big-time drug dealer."

"If he's a big-time drug dealer, he shouldn't be grabbing plums! Get your behind off of my fence!" That little piece of dirt out there, they can't sell drugs in front of it.

But everybody don't do that. When we help each other, we help everyone. It'll help your child and mine too.

I see them drive by here, drag racing up and down the street, and that frightens me. You could be in the middle of it when they do the drive-bys. Anybody could. Not sure what the answer is. Unless we find other things for the kids to get involved in.

My daughters don't want me to live here, but I don't want to move. I have good neighbors, I know them. I love my neighborhood. I've had that house since 1979.

I've got four kids. They're good kids. God was good to me, but I was hard on them. Couldn't nobody come to the house at all hours of the night looking for them, I did not allow that. When they got out of school, they had to come straight home. You can't stand on the corner somewhere. Come home or get involved. Then, they had to go and find a job. You cannot sit at home, and you cannot *not* go to school. If you don't want to go to school, go get a job digging a ditch—whatever you want to do.

My husband never paid child support. To buy the home that I have now, I worked three jobs. There was times when I sewed my shoes up because I needed to buy things for them. Yes, darn right I was strict on them! You have to be.

I'm glad my kids went to school out of the area. I sent my son to Menlo Park, there's a religious school. It wasn't easy with the little money I had to pay, but I sent him over there. I wanted him to meet and be around other kids. I always worried, if all you see is crime and you don't get to see how other people live, what do you have to live for? "Just because you live here in East Palo Alto," I used to tell him, "you don't have to do what other people do. You don't have to do that."

I'll never forget, it was 1981, I had Stanford students doing something here in East Palo Alto. Some kids—and this was almost unbelievable—were three and four years old, they had never seen white people before. At that time, this community was primarily a black community, probably 95 percent black. But still, I was just shocked. Just the fact of how isolated a lot of people were here.

There's been a change in this community: from blacks to Hispanics, a growing number of Pacific Islanders. Now you see a lot of the new homes are being bought by Asians. Three Middle Easterners came in the other day, their kids called me Grandma.

Over here in the clothes closet, sometimes, I have to stop people from fighting. Sometimes you're in the middle of three different languages, and saying, "Look, we're going to get along here. You guys can do whatever you want out there in *that* community but in *this* community, we're mainly women. We're supposed to get along, we're mothers. Let it start with us."

MARIA GUERRERO

We meet in her favorite local coffee shop: coffee, pastries, a TV on in the background. She grew up a few blocks away. Her parents bought a house soon after they emigrated from Guadalajara, Mexico: "They wanted something different for their five daughters. So we are fortunate to own a house, especially right now." She worked in the cafeteria at Intel, the semiconductor giant that remains an anchor of Silicon Valley today. There, she helped lead her coworkers to be among the first in the tech industry to unionize. She is coming from one labor rally and going to another after we meet.

dropped out of high school. To make more money, help out my family, I started working weird odd jobs. I started at Walgreens. I worked for a store called Factory to You. I was a stocker at Michael's. I did graveyard shift, from like two in the morning. But I got to put on my headphones. No one bothered me. It was kind of fun.

Then, I started working at Intel. At that point, I was working three jobs. I worked at Michael's from two in the morning to eight. Then I would take a nap for thirty minutes in the parking lot at Intel, go to work for about eight hours. I would get off at five thirty, drive to Factory to You. At six thirty I would start, and end at nine thirty. And then I'd go all over.

At Intel, I went from a coffee attendant to a cashier to the espresso bar.

I liked the foam art. I learned how to make a heart; I learned how to make bears; I learned how to make a swan, which was super difficult. You do a couple of strokes, then you go down, wiggle up, and then do the face. I did it once where it was amazingly perfect. I still have a picture in my phone.

Then I learned that if you add a little bit of color to certain things, you can make a Pikachu. The full-blown face of Pikachu in the coffee, yellow with the rosy cheeks. I made one for a customer, and she was super amazed, like, "I don't want to drink it, I don't want to ruin it!" Apparently, she drank it with a straw, so that the Pikachu would go straight down to the bottom. I made a coffee that says "Intel" on it. There's a picture of it hung on their fifth floor.

Customers would say, "I'm having a crappy day. I can't get this program to work." And I'd make the bear really quickly, hand it over, and see this big-ass smile.

And I enjoyed it. It was something new, something that I've never done before. But, you know, there were issues working there also.

At Intel, they have this system where you're either a blue

badge or a green badge. Blue badge, you're an engineer, you're a top admin. If you're a green badge, you're a subcontractor. Which means you're at the bottom. I was a green badge.

There's special events, like the end of the summer, outside with a carnival. If you were a green badge, you were not allowed to go to the picnic, not allowed outside. Since we made the food, we got to eat it anyways—as lunch. But we weren't allowed to go outside and play the games. You could only look. You couldn't touch.

They had it very separated—by class—as I liked to say, *segregated*.

Honestly, making those weird little coffees—that was a chance to do something different. Other than that, you were invisible. You were an invisible worker. Things got restocked magically.

There was this weird circle thing in the middle of the cafeteria that had the teas, the sugars, the lids, the coffee pots, the milk jugs, the soda machines, and the cups. Even in the middle of service, you had to go in between people to restock things. You couldn't get in. People would ignore you, reach across you, not say "Excuse me," not say anything. They just reached over you like you're invisible. They'd spill things and leave it. Or they'd say, "I dropped something," point, and walk away.

You're not allowed to say anything. You're not allowed to say, "Well, here's a towel. I don't have time because the coffee machine is overrunning." Nope. You had to clean it up.

Some people are just assholes. Excuse my language, but I mean people are. They see things, and they're just like, *Eh. That's not my job.* People have said to my face, "That's your job. Otherwise, why do we pay you?"

They were engineers and admin. We were below them. We were the help. You can't say anything, and you can't defend yourself.

There were problems with management too. One manager

just didn't like me. Everything I did was just wrong. She would get upset if I left something empty overnight after closing. She would take the person that would help me off my shift, so I'd be closing alone.

Then, there are certain issues that happen in any workforce. I don't want to say that a majority of them fall on *mujeres*, or women, but unfortunately, there's certain things that are said that can make you feel uncomfortable. A lot of people don't understand, that is a form of sexual harassment. They are just like, "Oh. Well, it is normal." Or, "It is natural."

I had a certain manager. He started out with jokes. Suggesting certain things or making comments that were double meanings. I would ask for a certain amount of coffee—because I worked at the espresso bar—and he would say, "Are beans the *only* thing you need?"

And I would just look at him. Maybe I heard him wrong. Maybe I took it wrong. So I'd make it clear, "Just the coffee beans. Five bags."

And he'd say, "Oh, I *bet* you need those. If you need anything else, just let me know. . . ." I didn't really know what to do or say, because it was my manager.

He would come to talk to me—it was just the two of us. He said, "Show me how you make this coffee." And when you have to show someone how to steam the milk, they have to be able to see it—it's a little too close for comfort. From then on, my coworker would make sure that he stood by my side, just so I wasn't alone.

Eventually, I told the manager that he made me feel uncomfortable. Of course he acted like, "I don't understand why you feel uncomfortable." Making me feel like it was all in my head, like none of that was true, or none of what I was feeling was relevant. And he would still keep saying things. . . .

So I was on the verge of quitting. I was getting panic attacks every day. My friend, he was a dishwasher. I told him, "I'm done with this place. I can't take this." I don't know how he understood me because I was crying, gasping for air, in the middle of a panic attack.

And he said, "Calm down. It's gonna be okay." He made me meet him the next day. And that's where they told me they were organizing underground.

I had never heard of a union before. I thought it was just for painters, construction workers, that kind of thing.

Then he started explaining what that meant: giving power to the workers, being able to stand up for yourself, without the fear of being fired, the fact that you have someone behind you. Not being scared. To me, that felt amazing—where I can actually be like, "You can't keep treating me like this!"

So I said, "I'm in. What can I do to help?"

He said, "Do you have questions? Concerns? Comments?"

And I said, "Nope. What can I do?"

I signed up to support the committee. I could reach people they couldn't, so soon I had my own little group that I could move. The more and more I heard, the more it fanned this fire that was already lit.

I had seen other people that were getting treated badly. But I learned so many people were getting discriminated against. Older-age workers written up for stupid reasons. There was only one person who was African American, he always got double the workload. You couldn't prove it, but you could see it.

People had been working there for, like, fifteen years and hadn't gotten a raise, a review even. The lucky ones might get a five-cent raise, fifteen, twenty-five cents. It's money, but when you have a family of four or a family of three, heck, even one kid or just a wife. . . . We're talking about a billion-dollar corporation that can't afford to help out.

These people never complained. If they got fired, what are

they gonna do? They have a family to feed. The worst thing was that after Intel, most folks would get off of work to go to another job, where maybe they'd get treated the same way.

I remember being at a meeting where they proposed doing a civil disobedience. One coworker wanted to do it, but she was in the middle of a custody battle with her ex-husband. Another coworker couldn't because of her papers and all that. And I said, "I'll do it. I don't have anything. I can get arrested for you." My friend Monica joined—we were the younger ones—"We're in."

I told my sisters, "I'm gonna get arrested in front of Intel." It turned into this huge thing. But eventually, my sister came around like, "It's funny to see you walk these steps, fighting for people's rights. Mom did the same thing." My mom was a housekeeper, but I'm learning she was also a big part of the community. She was this huge activist. She would go to rallies in front of City Hall. And she would call her friends and make sure people went because she saw how important it was.

Me and my mom used to butt heads a lot. The more you butt heads with your parent, the more you realize that you're just like them. When I was a kid and I got in trouble, she would say, "Did you start the fight?"

I said, "No."

She'd ask, "Did you finish the fight?" That was always her question. *Did you defend yourself?* She stood up for herself. She stood up for the people and the things that she believed in.

So we have this march in front of Intel. We take over the street. Ten coworkers, some janitors, some students, people from various organizations, a priest from a local church. The ones who planned to get arrested, we kneeled on the ground. Everyone else went onto the sidewalk. And we didn't move.

I got handcuffed. We got escorted onto the parking lot and got tickets for civil disobedience. Which was surprisingly fun! We were wearing these signs around our necks, and mine was flying around as we were getting handcuffed. It flapped up and hit me in the face, and I thought, *Hopefully there's no pictures of me like this. . . .*

Soon after, Intel offered us free health insurance. And a 20 percent raise. That was amazing—to *win*. After that, we decided to file for an election: all the workers at Intel who were eligible to join had to vote whether or not they wanted a union.

We went up as a committee—we rented a van, picked everyone up—to be present for when they actually opened the mail and got a count of the ballots.

It was very tense in that room. There were some nos that came out, a bunch in a row. Then two yeses and then another no. All of us were holding our breath. Just kind of like, *Oh my goodness. I can't believe this. We are gonna lose! How did we go wrong? Did we do everything right?* Then, at the end, all the yeses started coming in a bunch.

We looked at each other, we didn't want to get our hopes up. Some of us were trying to keep count. Some of us were like, "I'm not sure, I think I miscounted. Did we get enough yeses?" And as soon as we heard the final count, these big smiles came over our faces.

We started crying, thinking about everything that we had been through, everything that we had to endure. All that hard work, all the frustrations, all of the heartache, to see it actually come through in the end. We won.

We all started chanting, "*Sí, se puede!*" Or, "*Sí, se pudo!*" Which means, "Yes, we could!" The Labor Board's offices, they are library quiet, and here you have a bunch of workers with organizers just crying, and laughing, and chanting. Eventually they told us, "You all need to leave because you guys are too loud! Take it outside! Take it outside!"

The Unite Here Local 19. That is the union we won. It gives us a little more strength to be able to come out and defend ourselves. To say, "This is what is happening, and I need help."

We won quite a few things in our negotiation contract. We are getting a fifty-cent-an-hour raise every year. There is no one that makes less than $15 an hour there. We also won free health insurance for individuals—the union's health insurance, which is amazing. For families, they are only paying, I want to say, $80 a month, which is incredible compared to before. We are the first cafeteria workers ever to have won sabbatical in our contract. And on top of that, we have our three weeks' paid vacation. So in total, we can take up to six weeks off, paid.

I am now working full-time for the union, helping organize all these new places. I helped a little bit with the cafeterias at Cisco. I helped out with the Facebook campaign—546 workers. They just won a union and are in the middle of the negotiations.

We are seeing more and more support build in the tech community. The Intel fight had such a huge impact: we were so loud and public about what was going on that people were finally able to hear us. It struck people: gave them a sense of what was happening behind the scenes, made them see what wasn't so visible. It has been amazing to meet some of them, to share my story, and to see tech workers connecting with us.

The other day at Facebook, we needed some show of strength and power to help move the company, because it was kind of at a standstill. So, we decided to have the tech workers come in and stand in the background, just to show the company, *Hey, we support these cafeteria workers too. We stand with them. And we want to see them get better benefits.*

My optimistic self is hoping and praying that there is gonna be a lot more of us fighting that fight—more people who can find their voices and be able to say, "I want a union." Or "I want to help these workers." People who felt like I felt when I started, who didn't have a voice, who were getting panic attacks, who felt lost in life—they will say, "I found my strength." Because there is always going to be some kind of campaign, some kind of organizing, some kind of fight.

It's hard for me to wrap my head around everything that has changed. I started out working three jobs, the quiet, mousy person that let management step on me, make me cry, and give me panic attacks every single day. Now I'm this person who is going around and helping other people realize that they have that power inside of them, where they don't have to be so scared, they can defend themselves. It's hard to wrap my head around the fact that I set out this goal, and now I am an organizer!

And I am going back to finish my high school diploma. I literally have this semester, and I'm done. I'm excited. They have this little ceremony. I get to walk the stage if I want to.

It's a personal goal, and it's a family goal. Well, not a family goal—they would like me to finish, but no one was forcing me to go back. I finally felt, *It's time.*

My mom always was very upset that I didn't finish school. So I want to be able to feel like, *I finished, Mom.* I know her response would be, "It's about damn time." But she would have said it with a big-ass smile on her face.

ANDREW FREMIER

As a kid, he was always drawn to San Francisco—driving up from Carmel to see punk-rock bands in the early '80s. He remembers the old billboards and how they'd light up at night: "the

Sherwin-Williams paintball, the Coppertone girl with the suntan, the only one left is the Coca-Cola one, right?" When he graduated college, he got a job with the California Department of Transportation, doing minor repairs on the bridges in the Bay Area. It turned into a calling.

M*y connection to the Bay Bridge starts in 1987. I was fortunate* enough to work in what they call the Toll Bridge Construction Unit. We did minor repairs on the toll bridges because, at that time, there was no real plan. I had an opportunity to repair the Bay Bridge the first time in 1989.

I lived in the Mission. It was the World Series. I left work as quickly as I could, got to my house, turned on the TV, started watching the game, and experienced the earthquake firsthand. It was Loma Prieta.*

So I got in my car and drove to work.

The bridge was closed, and the cops were directing traffic off the bridge. I helped, and when the bridge cleared I got up and started working on repairs.

I worked about thirty or forty days straight after that. Nearly every span of the east end of the bridge had slipped from their seats and had to be jacked back into place. And there was substantial damage in the vicinity. Approaching the bridge, it was like a bunch of land mines had destroyed all the pavement in both directions, the soil just liquefied.

It's some of the best time in history, I think, when mankind is responding to an emergency. You get a lot of people *working together* instead of *working against*.

The Bay Bridge is what they call a lifeline bridge. It is sup-

---

* That earthquake, measuring 6.9 on the Richter Scale, caused over sixty deaths, nearly four thousand injuries, and an estimated $6 billion in damage. It became one of the most devastating and expensive natural disasters in US history and the largest earthquake since the 1906 quake that leveled the city.

posed to be open twenty-four hours after an earthquake, at least for emergency vehicles. So it represents so much in the transportation and growth of the Bay. It knits the Bay.

Before there was a bridge, in the '20s, there was a ferry system. The railroad ended in the East Bay, and people took ferries to get to San Francisco. The Bay Bridge first provided train service from the East Bay to the Trans Bay Terminal. Then, the interstate highway system started there: Eisenhower came out and proclaimed that we would connect the country from shore to shore. The bridge is part of that history. It's just always been that starting point for how you get to San Francisco.

But the old Bay Bridge sat on bay mud. It wasn't anchored into bay rock, except in a couple locations. The support system was Douglas fir timber from a hundred years or so ago. There was no real good connection between the timber supports and the concrete foundation. And it would have been very hard to make that connection sound. The steel that was used in the '30s is good steel, but they didn't understand the properties as well as we do today. So right, wrong, or indifferent, the decision back in the early '90s was to replace the old Bay Bridge with a new one.

It is a beautiful structure. Not just utilitarian, but iconic. It is amazing to see where you notice it. You can be driving on the Golden Gate Bridge and look to the left, and there it is. You can be at Pier 39, and the tower pops out over some of the wharfs out there. Take the ferry to Larkspur, and it comes out at some angles, pops out of the fog at night or glows gold in the morning. All the different times and weather conditions, subtle differences all day long.

It's beautiful. How many different perspectives there are and how things fit together. If you look down from the Berkeley Hills, you see this necklace of suspension bridges. With the Richmond Bridge and East Bay Bridge and the Golden Gate all off in that horizon. If you sit on the foot of one of those bridges, you get a very different perspective—how massive they are. From the bay, you can see the infrastructure in the water that you're not aware of when you're on top in a car.

The bay's given us these big, impressive, manmade engineering marvels that are so fantastic, from the bottom of the water to the top of the tower. I don't know, maybe that's my perspective because I've had the opportunity to climb them all and walk on them all and keep care of them all. I just find myself very attached to them and what they represent.

It's important for Bay Area residents to think about the nine counties as being all part of the same system.

For instance, every day I drive from Marin to Alameda County, across the Richmond Bridge through Contra Costa. So I drive through three counties every day. I spend a lot of time in the city of San Francisco. And I've got family on the peninsula and friends in Walnut Creek and in-laws that live in Santa Cruz.

My existence is probably representative of many folks in the Bay Area. Even if I don't live in many counties, I interact and take advantage of the benefits of all the others—and live with the problems of all of them also. So to me, it's obvious, as a Bay Area citizen, you can't focus all your energy on your own county and successfully navigate the adventures that the bay gives us.

But when we look at all the nine counties, they are all different. They have different opinions about economic change, about what land use means, in terms of the kinds of transportation systems that they have available to them and want to improve. About water. About taxation. About schools.

Just think how many different government agencies there are. You've got cities and transit agencies and counties and states and feds and permitting folks. They're all doing bits and pieces, but there doesn't seem to be a collective. There are twenty-seven different transit agencies in the Bay Area. Then you have tech playing a larger role, and other industries in the Bay have their agendas.

And so we face this periodic problem of balkanization in the Bay.

The big debate that we're having now is how to tie transportation and land use. There's a recognition that we need to make the transit system and the housing system work better together. It doesn't seem to be sustainable. You can't keep building out, out, and out and still have the same quality of life that we have today. You start to put all the other overlays on top of it, like water and power, all the other extremes that we've got to deal with—that stretching out of your supply line doesn't seem to make a lot of sense.

Our forecasts say that the Bay Area, which is now 7 million people, will be 9 million in twenty-five years. I don't know how you get enough water to 9 million people or how you build enough housing or how you get people around. So as much as people are concerned about their commute times today—how they get what they need or get where they need—it's gonna be a shock if we don't think about how those 2 million extra people are gonna fit in, assuming those projections are true.

Tech and government are very different. And their approaches to how fast things go are on opposite ends of the spectrum. Capital improvement, highway improvement, takes years. The industry represented by Google and Facebook, they don't see life that way. Things can't happen in years. So they hire buses, build their own park-and-ride facilities.

But the challenge is good for both sides. On the one hand, some of the bureaucracy that's involved in the slowness of a big public-works project is for the public's own good, because I certainly am supportive of our environmental restrictions and concerns. Time gives us the opportunity to educate the public and learn their needs so that we guarantee a good experience.

On the other hand, the public side right now seems to be very cash poor. There's not a lot of money floating around to make some of these investments. And the industry has a much different perspective on the availability of funds and the opportunity for decisive action.

So I think there's some good dialogue. A real opportunity to partner and maybe help them help us, and vice versa.

I do worry a little bit that there's a boom and bust happening. There's the changing landscape of the financial district, and how many large buildings are going there—exciting. The ballpark and the Warriors moving into town—those are all really positive signs for San Francisco. But I think San Francisco has to be careful. It could change too much, right?

There's a map of San Francisco. In fact, you can see it at City Hall, in the City Engineer's office. It shows legal streets that were never built. Development where they were gonna fill in the bay right south of Candlestick Point there and build a bunch of houses out in the middle of the bay.

San Francisco was going to be lined with freeways. It was gonna be a grid of freeways. The Mission Freeway. The 480 and 280 were supposed to connect. They were gonna have double Bay Bridges. There's all kinds of maps and development plans around that.

It's pretty amazing what would have happened if there wasn't pushback. Filling the bay to three feet above sea level. Building vast warehouses, industrial parks, and subdivisions across it and the hundreds of miles of salt ponds and hay fields surrounding.

The bay saved us. The bay is the magnet.

Think about San Francisco, the development of the waterfront. There used to be a highway that stretched along the Embarcadero and cut off the city from the bay. I was suspicious, but when they demolished it, what was left was amazing. Now you look at that open waterfront, and there's so much activity, physical activity, people running or walking and the little parklets that have been built on some of those wharfs. The view of the bridge from underneath, the lights. There's no shipping anymore—but the human connection to the bay is just fantastic.

Protecting the bay. It's not just about quality of life. It's about maintaining something. There's been a repeal of the advancement of man. A decision to exercise collective restraint.

Now the focus has been reestablishing the original ecological patterns. The return of nature. Turning the bay back into a marsh. It has made the area more beautiful even as we grow.

So it's been fascinating to be part of the changing shape of the Bay Area, even as just a small soldier. I've had an opportunity to touch every face of the bay, to shape the landscape for years to come.

PART VI

A SIXTH
SENSE OF
RIGHT AND
WRONG

n recent years, San Francisco's skyline has been redrawn: The new Salesforce Tower became the tallest peak downtown. It looms over everything that came before it and represents the new scions who've made San Francisco the western capital once again, attracting the admiration and sometimes the scorn of the rest of the nation.

From the top of the tower, you can see up to Marin, across the East Bay, and nearly over Bernal Heights to the peninsula. You can see the bay, the Berkeley and Oakland hills, the small townhouses lining up Russian Hill—but no people. The view tells a grand story, a shining El Dorado, finally discovered. But it's a story that neglects many of the characters at its feet. And from the top of that tower, the other golden city—the city of the Beats, of Harvey Milk, of Cesar Chavez, the one forged in the friction of diversity and conflict, the one that gave us new definitions for human dignity—that city seems submerged. For now.

Perhaps the right analogy for this time is not the Gold Rush but the Transcontinental Railroad. The train collapsed distance, made it possible for people to travel in days what once took months, and changed the country's sense of time. It was disorienting. Suddenly, California was no longer a distant frontier, but a close-tied part of a new American story. And let us not forget the blood and exploitation and pain that pooled underneath those tracks, the people who laid the steel, who fed coal into the furnace of the engine, who repaired the cars and hauled freight and waited patiently on passengers.

Today's technology has done something similar: distorted space and time, put San Francisco at the center of the world, brought us closer together (and yet we've never felt further apart). It sometimes feels as if we are *all* in the train's engine: The quicker things change, the faster we move to adapt, the hotter the economy gets, the more we are all getting cooked. A perpetual motion machine that will never bust.

But there has to be a way to free ourselves from the furnace. There has to be a way to unearth the forgotten city and breathe it back to life. To wash off the dirt and soot, to feel clean, and to see each other clearly again. If San Francisco has stood for anything, it is *that*: the ability—really, the necessity—to take dangerous risks in the name of an almost naked idealism. The city demands bravery, creativity, and also joy. It has proven time and again that we can imagine our way out of the prisons of our own making and conjure an impossible future.

KAREN CUSOLITO

In 1996, she moved to the Bay Area for what was supposed to be one year. Her mother had passed away, and the goal was to come to a place where she was anonymous. She stood on the coastline for the first time and could see for a hundred miles in all directions. "You just can't get that in New England. We have these tiny little squiggly coastlines and little tiny trees. Out here you've got redwoods. Everything is bigger and more open." So was the creative community in San Francisco, so much support and collaboration. She worked out of an abandoned warehouse in Oakland, the American Steel Studios, that she converted into an incubator for hundreds of other artists—until developers from New York bought the property and canceled her lease. She continues to move from space to space, studio to studio, searching for a new home that can handle the scale of her vision.

I am a large-scale industrial artist. I do large, fabricated steel sculptures that are as tall as forty-five feet, and weigh up to eleven to fifteen tons. Everyone comments, "How can such a small person make giant art?" A push of a button will move a ten-ton crane. A forty-foot boom lift will get me up to the top to work on things. There's no magic involved.

The scale of my work expanded when I got to the Bay Area. I was always interested in how things worked, how things were built. I went through a period of time where I was putting doorknobs on things that weren't doors. Just because I think art has a really powerful and playful ability to engage people about how they perceive things around them. I would watch people try to open a tree. They knew it wasn't going to open, but they still wanted to grab the knob and turn it.

Most of the work I do is built with salvaged steel. I've always believed nothing ever needs to get thrown away. It can always be turned into something or fixed. Minimizing my environmental footprint.

The Bay Bridge was always fascinating to me. It was built with steel from US foundries, and it was built with rivets that were forged by hand. One guy melting it, tossing it up to another guy, who drove it home. I mean, we just don't do stuff like that anymore.

It represented *possibility*.

When I heard it was going to be dismantled, I put a call out to the creative community: "What would you build with the steel from the Bay Bridge?" And I got drawings, sketches on cocktail napkins. I posted an online petition, and I got signatures and input from bus drivers, librarians, lawyers, welders. People from all walks of life—young, old, different ethnic groups, different classes, different levels of education, working in different kinds of industry—because it touched all of those lives.

It made me weep. One kid wrote, "I just want enough steel to make a picture frame for my grandfather who helped build that bridge." You feel how thick the passion is for this structure that unified everybody for so long.

The final meeting to get approval for the project, I remember sitting at the table and I showed them pictures: *Here is what people would build with this.*

And they said, "Karen, do you actually know how to build things like this, these big steel objects?"

I looked down. My nails are filthy. My hands are massive. And I said, "Yeah, I build big stuff." That was the day they gifted me a chromed rivet from the bridge. It remains in a place of prominence in my home.

I got to climb all over that bridge. It was like a dream. Up there, the "pedestrian passageway," as they call it, is just one cable that you hold on to. You don't get a harness. There's a 400- or 500-foot drop to the surface of the bay on one side and cars whizzing past at seventy miles an hour on the other. I was almost paralyzed, but I still was grinning ear to ear.

One of the engineers asked, "Why do you want this? It's just a piece of an I beam."

I said, "It is now, but once I get my hands on it, it will become something else." And I saw it click in his head, these shapes and forms that he had been working with for years, suddenly he was looking at them differently.

The steel went all over California. It went as far as the Mojave Desert. There have been installations across the state.

And I still have hundreds of tons. I keep moving it from space to space. But I envision some connective installation through and around the Bay Area with that steel. To encapsulate all of the shoreline around the Bay with this illuminated structure, forged from the steel.

Once I finish this project, I am hoping to just rent or buy a small RV and go cross-country. Go to these little towns, and go to the deserts and the mountains, and go get lost.

I remember a couple of years ago, driving out to Kings Canyon, and on the last stretch before you get to the foothills was this huge, single-story housing development, like a massive, cookie-cutter neighborhood, that was just abandoned. Empty streets, stores, churches, homes. It was just locked up. There was nothing.

I wonder, as the economy shifts, as many cities are becoming so similar, as the monoculture builds, whether one day we will abandon it too. If we don't hold on to everything that keeps these cities interesting, maybe they will be empty one day too.

PAMELA WEISS

Years ago, she walked into the San Francisco Zen Center, searching for answers: why she had lost her closest friend to a car accident, why she suffered from a chronic illness, why society felt irreparably fractured by race, culture, and religion. On the path, she became the first woman to have achieved "dharmic transmission"—the prerequisite to becoming a Buddhist priest. Today, she teaches the "dharma," or Buddhist teaching, as applied to modern life and encourages her students to walk the path of the bodhisattva, to become a "wise, feeling being."

The Zen answer cuts several ways across the current Bay Area narrative. It certainly asks some people to recognize their success is not going to cut it. It would also ask many people who lived here for a long period of time, who perhaps built a lot of the culture that made the Bay Area attractive to people, who may not have as deep a toehold in it as they once did, to sort of respect the temporariness of things a little bit. Basically we all need to be less busy putting up walls and trying to protect our stuff.

We can only do that in community. We heal through intimate relationship, through really getting to know each other, to walk in each other's shoes, to be personal. Because we all share the same roots: "us" and "them." I'm not over here, and you're not over there. I'm not right, and you're not wrong.

The piece that we have trouble with—we, humans—is that we have this binary brain that wants a yes-no, good-bad answer. And if we're willing to actually be in the fluid, alive, creative, sometimes scary and chaotic reality that is really unfolding, then it just doesn't work that way. So, the willingness and the ability to live with ambiguity, with not being so sure, this is really what "practice" gives us. It gives us a kind of grappling-in-the-dirt humility. And that is not an easy path, to be able to hold complexity and paradox like that. It's what the Buddha called "going against the stream." It's going against the stream of our own habits, and it's going against the stream of our culture. It's hard, but what else is there to do? Have a war?

Technology is like fire, right? It's neither good nor bad. It is whatever we use it for. We're probably not paying attention to the right problem or the right solution either. There's something to all this technology, too, that makes us need to wander the planet less and burn up less carbon. It may have answers that we don't realize. It's not like racism and police brutality weren't happening before. It's just now more of us see it. It's not that there weren't transgender people before, but now more of us see them.

There are a lot of bodhisattvas running around who are quiet. They're not famous. They don't have anything. They're not wearing a big T-shirt that says, I'M A BODHISATTVA. They're just people. They are people who are going about—as well intended as possible—doing good work in the world.

There's a story from the Jewish tradition about the Lamed Vov. "Lamed Vov" is High Hebrew; it's "thirty-six." And there's a myth that there always have to be thirty-six wise or holy—I think traditionally it was considered men—people on the planet maintaining the balance between good and evil. If there were less than thirty-six, then we would melt down into complete self-destruction.

But the thing is that nobody knows who they are. Everybody you meet could be one of these all-important people. In fact, you too could be one of these all-important people. You just don't know. Because not only are they invisible to others, but they're also invisible to themselves; the thirty-six don't know they are the thirty-six. And that's a beautiful way of thinking about how to hold the incremental, little pieces of good that we try to do in the world.

That radical reorientation of how we see the world—primarily how we see each other and the planet itself—I think that is what's needed now. It's not an easy thing. But it's happening all the time. There are people doing amazing things every moment. That stuff just doesn't get to the press. Maybe that person who is bagging your groceries, or clearing your table, or driving the bus, maybe he or she is also in that category. Maybe what we're doing really is important.

MICHAEL SANTOS

His favorite movie used to be *Scarface*, and in 1986 he was arrested in Miami for trafficking cocaine. During his twenty-six years in prison, he earned a bachelor's and master's degree, published fifteen books, saved over $100,000, and married the love of his life. He "returned to society" in 2012 and chose the Bay Area as his home. From California, he planned to start a movement, challenging the prison-industrial complex and teaching other inmates the skills that helped him to not merely survive but grow behind bars.

Everything I do is deliberate. *California was a deliberate choice. I was* about five years away from getting out of prison, maybe a little more, eight years away. Carole and I were on our plan. The revenues that I was generating from writing supported her so that she could go to school.

I said, "I don't have roots anywhere. You don't have roots anywhere. We're a prison family." I needed to go to the best possible place for me to start a career and have a meaningful impact on the world. California is an innovative, disruptive place. And you know I like the sunshine . . .

After twenty-six years, I was released on probation. Carole picks me up on August 13, 2012. I'm not free yet, I'm going to the halfway house in the Tenderloin, San Francisco. But I'm free as far as I'm concerned. The Tenderloin is Newport Beach, man. I do not care.

I'm stuck in there for a couple of days. I tell them, "Look, I know you're looking at the file. You're seeing I've been in jail twenty-five years, but I'm different. Don't take my word for it. Here are these letters." I had invitations to go to Stanford, to Berkeley. I had a job waiting for me. I had all these things. "I'm ready."

Three days later, I got a two-hour pass to go to the DMV. He said, "Are you going to take the bus?"

I said, "I'll run there."

"It's four miles."

"Dude, I can do it."

It was amazing. I ran to Fell Street. I ran the whole way, I was so excited. It was the first time I had walked without chains in society in twenty-five-plus years.

But I didn't know where I was going. I had to call my buddy and get him on Google Maps. He coached me the whole way, saying, "Turn here."

"Okay. I see it."

"Go right."

I wait in line. I pass the written exam—I had studied—but it's too late for me to do the driving. They said, "You got to make an appointment." Good thing too. I was so excited, I didn't realize I had forgotten how to drive.

I had some extra time, so I kept running, I was so happy. I ran to Burger King. Dropped $25, eating french fries, two Double Whoppers, a milkshake, Diet Coke, and more french fries. I just wanted an American cheeseburger so bad I couldn't wait. Let me tell you, a Whopper is priceless when you've been in jail as long as I have.

The next week, I get a pass to go out for my first day of work. I'm going to go meet Lee Nobmann, CEO of Golden State Lumber. We were both in prison; I worked with him every day on his book. He wrote a letter to the probation board that helped get me released.

He says, "Meet me at my office, and let's go out for lunch." Now, I'm not allowed out for lunch, right? So I'm not sure what we're going to do.

I get on the bus. There was a lady bus driver, and she could see how excited I was. I told her, "I just got out of jail after twenty-five years." She smiled, "My brother's in prison." I'm taking pictures with my iPhone. *My iPhone.* It's just an amazing experience.

I get off and go to Golden State Lumber. The secretary said, "Lee's got something special for you. But he's going to be another few hours. Just hang out."

I said, "Do you think my wife can come here? My wife is in the area, and I need to get a computer and stuff."

She said, "Yeah. By all means, do what you need to do."

Carole couldn't come to the halfway house, so this was the first time we were alone together. Ever.

I said, "Honey, I want to kiss you."

She said, "What if somebody comes in?"

"Honey, come on." We're like high school kids at forty, fifty years old.

When Lee got there, he said, "Let's go to lunch." I told him I wasn't allowed, and he said, "Oh, come on, man. Twenty-five years."

I said, "No, Lee. I got to stay. Do you mind if Carole goes and gets something, and we can just talk?"

We sit. Lee just looks at me and says, "What do you want to do? Don't tell me shit about prison. . . ."

I said, "I just want you to hear me out. I'd be an idiot not to honor your friendship and what you're offering me, especially considering my background. But I've been preparing for this for twenty-five years. I've got a story to tell. And I think it can do some good and really make a difference in the world. The prison system is the greatest social injustice of our time—"

He laughed when I said it. "*You* know that. *I* know that. But *nobody* cares except you and me."

I said, "Don't you think that's the reason I need to do this? Because it doesn't only affect people in prison and their children. It affects everybody in this office. The hundreds of billions of dollars that go to fund this monstrosity is taken out of health care. It's taken out of infrastructure. It's taken out of education. It's taken out of all of these other areas where it could have stronger use. I need to have a role spreading awareness. I can't do it without support. I don't want you to look at me as what I am right now. I want you to see where I'm going to be in five years. You were with me for nine months, and you saw how hard I work every day. I promise you I'll work even harder out here. You've just got to give me a little time, because I just need a job."

He said, "You come work for me, and we'll figure it out."

Every morning, I'd leave the halfway house at six and drive up to Petaluma. We'd talk business, talk over my plans. I used to give motivational talks at the office, practice public speaking. And I just started sowing seeds.

He financed my first house in a new development—helped me pick out all the appliances, all the granite, everything.

So when I left the halfway house, I drove Carole up to Petaluma. We walked into this beautiful, brand-new home. I'm taking pictures of her as she walks up the driveway, walks in the front door, telling her, "This is your house, honey. This is ours."

For want of a nail, I lost the war. But the reverse also works. If you take preparations, you're going to find people who believe in you. And when they support you, other things will open up too.

If we focus on building hope, if we focus on showing people their highest potential, people will aspire to that and strive. If we only tell people, "Maybe you can get a job," we're feeding the problem. This world needs to see success. It needs to see people do what nobody thinks is possible.

Last year, I took out a mortgage and started renting the place, took a tenant—we have people living there, paying for our retirement right now. I'm going to buy another house soon. I'm determined to do it. I'm not going to live in it. I'm going to rent it too, because I'm all about saving.

Carole jokes, "Why can't we live in our own house?"

And I say, "Honey, if I die, I want you to say, 'My husband took care of me.'"

OLIVER AND ALLEN

Oliver was born and raised in Northern California. He went to UC Berkeley and became a journalist who covered the AIDS crisis and helped shape the city's sense of its own identity. Allen is a son of the Midwest and a graduate of the seminary. He worked for a suicide prevention program and walked the Tenderloin at night in a clerical collar. They have lived together for forty years, most of it in the Castro, where they built a family together. San Francisco gave them a home, and, in a way, they did the same for others—not just in their careers, but as partners and fathers. We sit at the breakfast nook in their kitchen, surrounded by artifacts from their travels and photos of their family.

Oliver: We say that we probably saved each other's lives, by having a fairly—I mean, it wasn't totally monogamous—but we met in the '70s and were together and very involved from '78 on. And the AIDS crisis started in about '80, I think, '81. We had to be more responsible with each other.

Allen: We met at a cocktail party—we were both in Puerto Vallarta at the same time—kind of a gay cocktail party that was given by someone—

Oliver: It was given by a Catholic priest. Oh, what was his name? He picked me up. I was buying postcards on the street. Only later did I find out he was a priest, when he wanted me to go to the Epiphany mass with him. [*They laugh.*]

Allen: Oliver lived in Oakland. I lived in San Francisco. I invited him for dinner. And he stayed for a week.

Oliver: At first, we kept our places, but we would go back and forth. And then—I guess about a year after we met—you moved to the Haight where I was living.

Allen: We eventually moved to this place in the Castro in 1989.

Oliver: And have been here ever since.

Allen: We traveled a lot. We always loved Mexico—Latin culture—the Andes when we went to visit. We went to Ecuador, Argentina, and Brazil.

Oliver: We always used to joke with our friends in Puerto Vallarta that we were Mexicans trapped in gringo bodies.

Allen: We went to Peru and that is how we met Teresa, who is the mother of our daughters. She and her boyfriend were coming to the States to visit her sister, who was already living in Kentucky. We told them, "You guys should come out and visit us!" We had an extra bedroom. So they came—

Oliver: On the Greyhound bus. They showed up at our front door in the Mission—

Allen: Dressed in tribal—

Oliver: Total indigenous Andean outfits.

Allen: It was exciting to have them in town.

Oliver: We did the whole thing up. We took them to *Beach Blanket Babylon.*[*]

Allen: The two of them stayed for a month or two.

Oliver: Teresa eventually got a job as a housekeeper. The boyfriend had to go back to Peru, because he had family down there. He and Teresa became very estranged. And then, nine months later, we learned that Teresa was pregnant. Unbeknownst to us.

Allen: She visited us every weekend.

Oliver: But she would wear her outfits, and we had no clue she was pregnant. She called me up and told me she was in the hospital. And I said, "Did you get hit by a truck or something?" And she says, "No, *tengo* baby." And I'm going, "You're kidding!"

Allen: So we rushed over there.

Oliver: Picked up her and the baby and brought them back the next day. I said, "Most people have nine months to prepare for this. I've had a day and a half. Do you have an operating manual?"

Allen: It's easy to fall in love with a baby. We helped name her. Clara.

Oliver: And we said, "To hell with it. You can just stay with us."

Allen: That just evolved into our feeling like we were a family.

---

[*]   A campy musical revue that has performed in North Beach for more than twenty-five years.

Oliver: It was pretty easy for us, because Teresa was like Supermom.

Allen: She really was a saint.

Oliver: She took good care of everything. For us, it was just, "Goo goo, gaga"—you know, play-play kind of thing. It didn't seem as difficult as it might have been.

He shows a photograph. The family: a woman at the center holding a baby, two men, one on each side. Oliver has a phenomenal late-century moustache.

Oliver: Years passed, we lived together. Clara was in school, probably five or six. And Teresa suddenly says, "I have to go back to Peru." She had an older daughter, Rita, still there. "If I don't, she will end up sixteen years old and pregnant, and I'm not going to have that." And we're going, "Well, you can't leave us. You just can't pick up with Clara and go off!" Because we were all pretty well attached by then. And so we hatched a scheme that Allen and Teresa would get married.

Allen: We talked to an immigration lawyer first. We brought Teresa and Clara. We said, "We are already a family. We just want to add Rita and we don't know what to do." And the lawyer said, "You know, people get married for a lot of different reasons." He and his law firm would support us. But he said, "Be sure to have your mother at the wedding!"

Oliver: We brought Allen's cousin, who is a minister, over from Iowa. We had a full-scale wedding in a neighborhood church.

Allen: It wasn't a religious wedding, the church was a backdrop.

Oliver: We had a big reception at a restaurant nearby.

Allen: We invited about twenty friends. And my mother came.

Allen shows another photo of him tall and in a white tuxedo standing next to Teresa. Oliver stands nearby. They are all smiling.

Allen: The whole process getting Rita over took months. We had to arrange the wedding. We needed to legalize Teresa, because she was here illegally too—she had come on a student visa. And then we could bring Rita: family reunification, you know, the whole thing.

Oliver: We had to go back to Peru and do this all at the American embassy.

Allen: We had a little interview. It was at a bank window with some young staffer. And he asked me two questions: "Were you married in a church?" and "Does your wife have a ring?" And of course, we were married in a church—it was right on the wedding certificate. And on the way to the interview, Teresa stopped and bought a ring, because she thought that maybe she needed one.

Oliver: I was staying nearby. They came back and told me all of this. And of course I went into a total rage, saying, "What business is it of the State Department of the United States whether you were married in a church or not?!"

Allen: When we came back to Miami from Peru, they pulled Teresa aside and asked her all these questions about my mother and my father. Well, of course, she had the answers—she had met them—and they consider her part of the family too.

Oliver: When Rita got here, we sent her to Newcomer High School—San Francisco schools had a program where they bring all of the immigrant kids. They had Filipino, Chinese, Latinos, European kids, everybody. Seventeen different languages, and they throw them all into this one high school and do English immersion. And it worked like a charm. Within a year and a half, she was perfectly fine.

Allen: She went to UC Santa Barbara. She and her husband

bought a house in Marin. Now she works at a Bay Area foundation.

Oliver: To raise a child from another ethnic group, that is a real eye-opener. They were very dark-skinned, especially as little girls. And the school assumed a lot of things. They assumed Clara didn't speak English and put her in the remedial classes. English was her first language, and we had to straighten them out. Even then, they would look at me and wonder where she came from. There were a lot of comments about "Who is she?"

Allen: Teresa was a constant presence. And she is really an indigenous activist.

Oliver: She is involved in community groups in the Mission.

Allen: She knows Carlos Santana, the musician. She knows Rigoberta Menchú, a famous human-rights activist from Guatemala. She was the main force in keeping the language and the culture alive in the family. We go back to Peru every couple of years to visit and see all the cousins. I mean, we feel like they're our family too.

Oliver: But it's interesting. Clara, born in San Francisco, raised in the Castro, is more attuned to her background and culture than Rita is. Rita is moving on. From a hut high in the Andes to an Eichler* and a Prius. She has a five-year-old daughter, and she is not teaching her Spanish.

Allen: But Clara kept up her Spanish really well. She works at a tech company, but every Saturday or Sunday she works at a street fair in the neighborhood.

Oliver: A little bazaar. Clara has a booth there, and she sells stuff that the family sends up from Peru.

He shows me a photo: Oliver, Allen, and Teresa, in the center. To their right, Rita, her husband (who is incredibly tall), and their daughter in their arms. To their left, Clara smiling broadly.

---

* A style of midcentury-modern house ubiquitous in Northern California.

Allen: We started a family before it was fashionable. We still send Christmas cards out with pictures of our family.

Oliver: We encourage the kids to stay in touch with their father in Peru, but Clara doesn't even recognize him or speak of him.

Allen: She said, "I only have two dads, you and Oliver."

SAAD KHAN (CONT'D)

Perhaps in part because he spent much of his childhood in Pakistan, something challenged him to ask the hard questions of the tech industry and push his work in it to serve the right mission: "Getting off of a plane from Karachi and driving into San Francisco—or going back—it was always a bit of a phase shift. It gave you a sense of the bigger world out there and that there's a lot of people in the Valley not connected to it. So how can technology affect that bigger world? And how can we get the means of production in the hands of as many people as possible?" Starting his own firm, he has become a bridge figure between Silicon Valley and the rest of the world and works to put the industry's vast resources and creativity to the world's most urgent challenges.

I t was always clear that the kinds of problems you could go after could be infinite.

Having grown up abroad, I saw this whole other world that was not being served—and if you looked in the right way, it was a really interesting market opportunity. I could see how much energy there was—and how much talent there was—untapped both here and in other parts of the world. It maybe was an obvious thing for me, but it wasn't necessarily obvious to a lot of other people.

I started teaching a little bit at the design school at Stanford. I was an industry guest a couple of times at a class called "Designing Liberation Technology"—seeking creative solutions, for example, in parts of the world without electricity. The d-school was a magical place for people who are empathetic (empathy is a staple in "design thinking") and applying it to different kinds of opportunities. It felt like home for me.

Then, through a series of coincidences, I started teaching in the Middle East. I wrote this piece that was called "Why the Arab World Needs Heroes." And it happened to get published five days before the Arab Spring started, totally coincidental. I was watching these events unfold on a world stage, and I got the call from a friend of mine, "Hey, you should come talk about this at the State Department." It was surreal. My topic was the political implication of social media, and the day of my talk, President Mubarak stepped down in Egypt.

I was the right person at the right time, I suppose. The next thing I know, the State Department was like, "Hey, we want someone to host and mentor this start-up weekend in post-revolution Egypt, and USAID will fund it." I mentored at a developer conference with Google in Saudi Arabia. The government of Malaysia invited Silicon Valley to come—it was an event for local entrepreneurs called "Silicon Valley Comes to Malaysia"—and so I went. I even got the opportunity to meet the president of Turkey.

During this period, there were many "small world" moments. One entrepreneur I met at the start-up weekend in Egypt, he was nineteen at the time. He had way too much swagger for somebody his age. A year and a half later, I get a call from one of my CEOs at a hot venture-backed stealth start-up in the Valley. And he's like, "We finally found our guy."

I said, "Sure, tell me about him."

And he's like, "Oh, he's from Egypt, and he said he met you at this event there years ago. He remembered your conversation." Turns out the same kid had managed to find his way out to the Bay Area, within six months had this place completely wired, and was now debating whether he should take this job at this cool start-up or start his own. Ultimately, he decided to start his own. And I wrote him a check.

But more importantly, you felt like these conversations were having a real impact on people. You connected to actually making a difference in someone's life. I came back from trips, and I was like, *What is the point of having all these resources—being alive when we are, where we are—if we're not doing something that matters?* So that took me down this whole new path.

I started taking a species-level view on a lot of things. (You can only do that if you're in certain places in Maslow's hierarchy.) And there are a lot of things that are happening in the Valley that feel like they will have species-level implications: from a health perspective, from a genome perspective, in research labs, changing how we work, think, move, how long we live.

I was spending time with two friends of mine, one who was in my freshman dorm at Stanford—we had all been thinking about this. What are the products and services that feel like they're actually additive, that are environmentally friendly, and what are business models that are aligned with these values? How do we get the smartest people—the same thinking that made Airbnb and Lyft—working on the most important problems?

My thesis used to be, *Just bet on good people, and everything else works itself out.* But I started thinking, *It's not just about good people, we also gotta think about the real values behind what they want to do.* And guess what? When you get the world's best people working on really meaningful problems, pretty amazing things happen.

We met Ben Rattray, a guy who was very much focused on citizen engagement as today's single biggest challenge for democracy to function: How do we build an informed populace that can actually have an impact from the ground up on whatever issues that they care about? That's what he wanted to make.

We raised a fund to invest in his company. It took a few weeks. Came back and said, "Okay, here's your check." We were the first institutional investors alongside Pierre Omidyar's fund to support Change.org.

And word got around.

We didn't know how many more companies like this there might be. But it turns out, there were a lot. The next thing I know, lots of other people are talking, "Hey, we've heard about you guys and what you've done."

And on the other side, we didn't know how much money would be available for these kinds of things. But it turns out some of the biggest, deepest, well-known pockets in the world—some pretty awesome people—had gone through their own personal evolution.

So fast-forward to today. We've deployed tens of millions of dollars in a portfolio of companies run by some of the best people in the world, animated by values, tackling problems worthy of their lives. And we're seeing it in the returns. When you marry all those things together, you don't get a handicapped company or a "social venture." You get the potential for the best companies in the world.

And that's what we're on a mission to prove now. That there's no reason that you can't have your cake and eat it too. You can work on the biggest problems in the world, and not just build businesses but, in fact, be conscious world leaders too.

In Silicon Valley, you gotta have one example of something that works, and then the momentum builds. At this point, we have lots of companies that are executing this way and we think are going to be successful—if they're not successful already. They employ a lot of people, and they train a lot of people. Those alumni are going to go and start their own companies—up the game for everyone. That's how this starts.

We are helping build the future not just for our families, or local communities, but often the world. So I feel a big responsibility to do it right. If you think the inequities are bad now, they can get drastically worse. So the need for responsible stewardship is greater than ever. And so much is contingent on whether we do it right or not.

There are no silver-bullet answers. Better economic opportunity, better mobilization of local resources, better housing, justice. Frankly, these are not problems that the Valley is good at solving. At least historically, it hasn't been. The market has failed, our public institutions have failed. And people have a right to be angry.

But there is an awakening of consciousness that's happening. For me, it's about how do we get resources into the people's hands who are going after meaningful problems. And let them experiment and figure some of these things out. Let them come up with the models for the future, new institutions, new tools. Help them build cultures around that kind of thinking, and that kind of empathy, and hold them accountable.

And let's see—I bet we can take back capitalism and remake it in our image.

EDWIN LINDO (CONT'D)

In April 2016, two officers fired seven bullets, killing a forty-five-year-old homeless man named Luis Góngora after he rushed at them with a knife. By many counts, this was the twelfth death in two years that resulted from the San Francisco Police's excessive use of force—deaths that may have been avoided had officers followed proper protocol, deescalated the situation, or just been less quick to pull the trigger. For all its liberal bona fides, San Francisco was part of a national epidemic of police violence against minority communities. In response to the killings, Edwin Lindo and four others began a hunger strike outside the Mission Police Station, calling for the resignation of police chief Greg Suhr and demanding widespread reform. And stories about protests in San Francisco, once again, traveled nationwide.

We just got a new name. "The Frisco Five." We love the name. It's only white people that hate the name Frisco. Black and brown people, we love it. The Frisco Low Riders were the original low riders.

We're on day thirteen. For me, day fourteen—I stopped eating the day before. We came here with five chairs. I haven't changed or showered. And all of this was donated to us. All of it. These tents were donated, chairs were donated, umbrellas because the first night it rained and our bodies were soaked, all we had were our blankets to cover us.

It's a response to a breaking point. Continuing seeing black and brown people taken indiscriminately—the value of the human body that has melanin so diminished—relatives and friends who live around the corner from me—holding the hands of the parents, knowing they will never see their son again. It could have been me. It could've been my daughter.

All in the "most progressive city in the country." Progressivism is a veil, and we're trying to rip that veil apart. How can you be progressive and have 25 percent unemployment in the Mission for people of color? The irony is we are going hungry in a city that has starved our community for decades.

We're taking back the power of our humanity, the value of our bodies. We will no longer allow you to destroy our bodies; we're doing it ourselves. And all of a sudden the gun is meaningless, the policies are meaningless, because we're saying, *You don't have the power to hurt us.*

We've had thousands of people. Yeah, thousands of people come here every single day. Bringing us broth. Books. Talking to us. People are honking every minute. We have second graders writing us letters of support. We have college students who are sleeping here at night to watch over us. The homeless have stayed with us. Tech workers have sat down with us and said, "What do I need to do to let colleagues know what's happening? Because I know they will get behind you." All kinds. They've hung out, they've come, they've gone. This is community living. This is a community space.

Al Jazeera did a video. It has 1.2 million views. Lebanon did a piece on this, Egypt, Rome, Tokyo. The biggest newspaper in France. I mean, I got a text message from someone in South Africa, saying, "We stand in solidarity with you." Harvard Law School had a contingent with sign that said, WE STAND IN SOLIDARITY WITH THE FRISCO 5. University of Washington, the law school I went to, the dean wrote a letter to Ed Lee, saying, "You will not let an alum of mine die, you need to fire Chief Suhr." She sent an email to the entire student body, saying, "This is the type of leadership we need in our country. This is not people sitting on the street for a publicity stunt. This is shaking the consciousness, people willing to put their lives on the line for justice." Shaun King sent me a message and said, "Brother, you are our heroes." And I don't know what that means—I haven't left this block in thirteen days.

My dad . . . at first, he was . . . he was supportive—just on principle . . . it's his son doing it. Then, we got into day four and five, and he got scared. I had passed out and collapsed. My blood sugar went down. I think it was the shock. Ambulance came . . . and my dad's like, "You gotta go. I'm going to take you now."

But I said, "No, no."

"Son, this guy, this mayor will let you die here."

And, I said, "Dad, we have it, we have him."

Then, on day nine, he came back, and he said, "Son, I will be here every night. I had a revelation. You're cleansing this city by cleansing your body. 'Cause what's happening in this city. See, the people that are running this city are committing genocide." He meant the gentrification and displacement, the bad education system, and the killing and imprisoning of people. And he said, "So it took a while but I understand what you're doing. There's going to be some pain because these people, you've called their bluff."

This has become a spiritual journey. Last night, I didn't feel the concrete was below me. I felt like someone was holding me up. Where I walk, I don't feel the earth, I feel like I'm floating. I've got to the point where I've realized that the purpose of our bodies is to be the vessel to carry our minds. I'll be honest, your senses get heightened, and I feel people now. I see through people—their energy, that's what I see now—I see their heart.

I meditate a lot. Before, I'd have all these thoughts running, and the first part of the meditation is to just clear my mind. I don't have that anymore. I close my eyes, and I get to this point of connection, and it's . . . it's euphoric. And this process showed me that we live in a gluttonous world. Everything we do is excess. This process removes all the toxins. I haven't felt hunger in four days. My body's weak. And it puts the world in perspective. Choosing hunger is a privilege, a blessing, because it means I had something to eat before. There are people on the street that are in this state every day.

Things were going to stay the same—in this city, in this country—unless we shook up the consciousness. I think I'm put on this earth to make people feel uncomfortable. Because when people are uncomfortable, that's when they change.

Democracy is not stale, it is a living thing. It has to innovate. Governance has to innovate. Policing, schools, structures, systems have to innovate.

People need to know that this city is back to the people. People need to know that they can make an impact. People need to know that they can run this city and hold elected officials accountable. The city, the country, needs to know that the people can win. We're going to show the world a different way.

That's why this all had to come back to where it started. To the Bay Area. Where the Black Panthers formed. Where the Brown Berets were formed. To Cesar Chavez, to Harvey Milk. To the protesters that got us these public spaces and these parks and fought for ethnic studies at SF State. To the resistance, the culture that people were attracted to.

The city is something special. It raises people who seek justice. It provides you a sixth sense of what's right and what's wrong. And there aren't many cities like that.

CODA

DAN ZELINSKY

He slides up on roller skates, a wrench in one hand, the other stretched out for a handshake. We're standing in a warehouse at the end of a pier at Fisherman's Wharf. Outside, there is a line of old seafood haunts, each with starched tablecloths in back, fried clams and shrimp out front. Inside the warehouse, we are surrounded by old coin-operated arcade machines: player pianos, games of strength and skill, mechanical fortune-tellers, fantastical diorama—all of which come to life for only a quarter. We meet next to a machine called Cactus Gulch, where the Old West is frozen behind glass until someone drops a coin in the slot.

t was in my basement growing up as a kid. My dad always had antique coin-op all around. It was his passion. He just loved antique machines that would do incredible things when you dropped in a coin.

I was always tinkering with my dad. While he was tinkering, I was, I guess, un-tinkering, taking things apart. Dad got pretty good at putting things back together. And I never really paid much attention until I started working at one of my dad's arcades—that was in 1972.

Eventually all the employees starting retiring and passing away, guys that my dad hired to do all the repairs. And then I noticed I had a lot of broken stuff. It got to the point where if I didn't know how to keep this stuff working, none of it's gonna work.

[*He looks around, pats down his jean pockets.*] Let's talk about how easy it is to lose a tool when you haven't taken one step in any direction. You put it down and then you go to pick it up, it's not there! I drive myself crazy.

Now my whole thing is make 'em work like they originally did. So I buy a lot of original parts. And *battle, battle, battle.*

I'm still here, I'm happy. I think it's been sixteen years, every day. I'm set in my ways, and my course is really dedicated to keeping old-school things up and running. Modern day has nothing to do with the old school, so I'm kind of alone doing this and trying to present it to whoever happens to meander in.

[*He points to an mechanical arm-wrestling machine called the Golden Arm.*] This one wins a lot. You get two plays, so you can hurt yourself twice for only a quarter.

The city is changing—whether it's good, bad, or indifferent. I'm getting older. I've traveled, but I'm comfortable here. I don't really have a reason to live somewhere else. And this is a major sanctuary, so it's my passion. I'm just trying to keep machines working every day and make as many people as happy as I can, because that's what's happening to me.

Tech is a fad that will wear out, and everything makes a

comeback in time. That's why antiques are sought after. So let them play with their new toys, let them get old and boring. Kids that are into their modern games come in here and they're intrigued by it, because they actually get to interact with something mechanical. Not a common event anymore.

My favorite part of the collection is the music. There's great music here. Best way to start if you're gonna learn how to play the piano, just listening and watching the keyboards go. That's how I learned. I can now play most things by ear, and I play a lot of ragtime.

[*He points across the room.*] See the three or four people standing there? They're having a blast! They're enjoying that piano for one quarter. That's pretty damn cool.

Admission is free. The doors aren't closed to anybody. There's a lot of weird people when you're open to the public. Oh my God! But I find that what they really want to do is enjoy any moment of their day, as much as anybody else. They come in here after panhandling sometimes, and they get to play the machines that they grew up with. They're having a blast. I'm not taking that away from them, no way.

People walk in here and all of a sudden the nostalgia nerve gets struck. Because they grew up with this stuff as kids. They were playing it with their grandparents, or their parents, so the history is kept alive. They are just like kids again. I mean, nostalgia is a real powerful drug.

It's crazy. This lady came in, my age, really old. She comes in with her daughter and she remembers Laughing Sal from Playland. And she says, "I've got to play this for you!" Her daughter is maybe six. "This is the best thing from my childhood. This is the best!"

And the daughter is just all excited. She starts Laughing Sal, and her kid is terrified. She hides behind her mom, and she's yelling, "Mom! Are you sure this is fun? Let's go!" And her mom is going, "Yeah! This is great! Isn't this great?" She goes, "No! Mom, let's go home!"

So times may have changed, but that machine has terrified kids for decades.

Acknowledgments

This project grew from my own community. It began as part of my graduate studies at Stanford University. My thanks to so many colleagues and mentors who helped nurture the seed in its early days: Larry Marshall, Joan Petersilia, Michelle Anderson, Norman Spaulding, Jan Martinez, and Cathy Glaze. Thanks also to Anna Nelson and Claudia Dreifus for teaching me to love the interviews.

Then it was raised by friends: especially Richard, whose faith in the project was blind and steady. My gratitude to Ahmad, Alexandra and Murphy, Alexis and Anna, Ares, Arwen, Barry, Basho, Ben, Bill, Brett, Brücius, Cameron and Tatiana, Cheryl, Christian, Christen and Mark, Curtis, Daniel, David, Dean and Clary, Deborah, Deirdre, Elis, Eliza, Emily and Mark, Eric, Fred, Gary, Gerald, Greg, Heather and Andrew, James, Jamie, Jess, Jesse and Gavri, Jim and Shirley, Joe, John, Joy, Kahlil and Ashley, Kari, Kat, Kate and Tom, Kelsey, Kim and Brian, Kristen, Laurel, Leez, Leslie and Kyndall, Linda, Liz, Lorenzo, Lucia, Matt, Marijeta, Mark, Marta, Michael, Min, Nadia, Nigel, Nikki and Gab, Omid, Paul, Pete, Rachel, Reihan, Sadia and Andreas, Sam, Sara and Mike, Sarah and Roy, Stephen, Teresa, Troy, Victoria, Veronica, and Wes for inspiring me along; Aysha, Cat, David, Karin, Matt, Megan, Rafay, and Susan for lending fresh eyes; and Alex, Bridget, Marilyn, Richard, and Rob for giving me somewhere to call home in San Francisco once I had regrettably moved away. I feel very lucky to have worked with Kristina at Wylie and Matt and Remy at Norton, all of whose support and insight refined this book more than I could ever have done alone.

Special thanks to family in all things: my parents, Stephanie and Carter, for their shoulders; my brother, Spencer, for his mind; and my in-laws, Jean and Larry, for their instincts and honesty. Also to my grandparents Helen and Mitch Palmer for laying the family's roots in the city of San Francisco.

Above all, thanks to my wife, Lisa. For teaching me how to build a home after years of being nomadic. For holding my hand when we walk down the street and seeing the same strange world I see. And for teaching me to love the region that raised her.

We have a son, his name is Harris, and he taught me what it means to be present: it is to remember that we are led and succeeded by people greater than ourselves.